COMBAT COLOURS No.2
The Hawker Hurricane
in RAF, Commonwealth and FAA service 1939 – 1945
by H C Bridgwater
artwork by Peter Scott

INTRODUCTION

The Hawker Hurricane entered service with the Royal Air Force some eighteen months before the start of the Second World War and was still on 'active service' at the end of the conflict. It can be said that the Hurricane fought in more campaigns, on more fronts, and in more countries and Theatres than any other British fighter during that war. This particular volume covers the camouflage schemes and markings carried by Hurricanes, in a variety of different Marks and sub-types, which served with the RAF, Commonwealth and Fleet Air Arm squadrons between September 1939 and August 1945.

Because of the scope of the subject, the coverage given here is of necessity relatively brief. Much research is still going on into the finer details of the aircraft camouflage and markings used by the RAF and FAA during the Second World War period, so it is perhaps inevitable that some of the information given here may subsequently need revision. That said, the contents of this book reflect the extent of our collective knowledge of this subject at the present time of writing.

I am indebted to Paul Lucas for sharing some of his research with me; to Peter Scott for his excellent artwork; Andrew Thomas, Dick Ward and Ian Carter for the photographs, and to the series editor, Neil Robinson who exercised great patience and tact whilst convincing me that I could indeed write something of this nature.

H C Bridgwater
Luton
August 2001

Scale Aircraft Modelling
Combat Colours No.2

'The Hawker Hurricane'
by H C Bridgewater

Artwork by
Peter Scott

Series Editor: Neil Robinson
Design and layout: Steve Page

Published by Guideline Publications
352 Selbourne Road
Luton Bedfordshire LU4 8NU
Tel: 01582 505999

www.samnet.co.uk

Contents

Camouflage and Markings in the European Theatre of Operations — Page 2

Camouflage and Markings in the Middle Eastern Theatre of Operations — Page 48

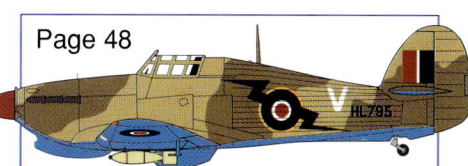

Camouflage and Markings in the Far Eastern Theatre of Operations — Page 52

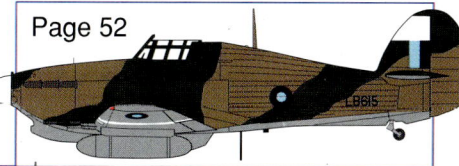

Camouflage and Markings of Fleet Air Arm Hurricanes and Sea Hurricanes — Page 54

Below: Epitomising the Hurricane's camouflage and markings in its finest hour, this classic shot of a Gloster-built Hurricane Mk I, P2798 LK·A of 87 Sqn., circa August/September 1940 at the height of the Battle of Britain, flown by (then) F/Lt Ian 'Widge' Gleed, shows an otherwise standard Dark Earth/Dark Green uppersurface and Sky or Sky Blue undersurface scheme, with 'oversized' 49 inch diameter fuselage roundels, (created by adding an additional Yellow outer ring to the original factory applied 35 inch diameter Red/White/Blue roundels), all-red leading edge to the fin and red propeller spinner. Note the overpainted serial number. (Andrew Thomas Collection)

HURRICANE CAMOUFLAGE AND MARKINGS IN THE EUROPEAN THEATRE OF OPERATIONS

The Hawker Hurricane was the first of the RAF's new breed of monoplane fighters to enter service. Designed to Specification F.36/34, the prototype made its first flight on 6 November 1935 and entered service with 111 Sqn at Northolt in December 1937. By the time World War Two began in September 1939, the RAF had sixteen Hurricane squadrons fully operational with one more in the process of working up.

The camouflage scheme applied to the Hurricane in September 1939 had been developed at the Royal Aircraft Establishment at Farnborough during the early 1930s where it was termed the Temperate Land Scheme.

This Temperate Land Scheme, as applied to monoplanes, was made up of two colours named Dark Earth and Dark Green which were applied to the upper surfaces in a disruptive pattern intended to break up the outline of the aircraft when viewed from above at altitudes of 10,000ft or less.

There were two distinct patterns of this disruptive scheme applied to the aircraft on the production line known as the 'A' Scheme, and a mirror image, known as the 'B' scheme. The uppersurface colours extended down the fuselage sides to the lower longeron.

The undersurfaces of new aircraft were finished on the production line with the port side of the aircraft painted in Night and the starboard side in White - the two colours meeting down the centreline of the aircraft. This was done to allow the Observer Corps to positively identify British fighters whilst they were over land, and to facilitate tracking of 'friendly fighter' formations as the radar system then in use did not extend in to inland areas. Some aircraft which had been in service before the 'black and white' markings came into use, only had the undersurfaces of their mainplanes finished in this manner with the tailplanes, rear fuselage and engine cowling underside remaining in the original painted Aluminium.

Hurricanes were initially fitted with a Watts two-bladed wooden propeller, the blades of which were painted Night with Yellow tips with the metal spinner cap in Dark Earth. When the variable pitch three-blade de Havilland propeller, and later constant speed Rotol propeller, were introduced and fitted, they were also painted Night with Yellow tips and with Night spinners.

Generally speaking, the National markings consisted of Red and Blue roundels on the upper surface of the wings, in which the Red centre was 2/5ths of the overall diameter of the roundel with a similar roundel on the fuselage sides. The exceptions to this rule were aircraft manufactured by Glosters which appear to have marked their Hurricanes with Bright Red and Bright Blue roundels until at least September 1940. Other aircraft manufacturers are also thought to have been guilty of this practice, but at the moment, the culprits remain unidentified.

Identification markings took two forms. The first was the aircraft's serial number which remained with the aircraft throughout its service life. This was applied to the rear fuselage in 8 inch high characters applied in Night. There was no standard form of characters used, with each aircraft manufacturer having its own style. The second identification marking took the form of three letters, which were applied to the sides of the fuselage, in Medium Sea Grey. Two letters were used to identify the squadron, and a single letter served to identify the individual aircraft within that squadron. The two squadron letters were always placed together on one side of the fuselage roundel, whilst the individual aircraft letter was placed by itself on the other side of the roundel. The two letter squadron code could be placed on either side of the roundel. These letters were supposed to be 48 inches high, but in practice many different sizes were used. As with the serial number, there was no standard style to these letters, with almost every squadron using a different style from the others.

It is often said that no plan survives contact with the enemy, and it was not long after the outbreak of war that the Air Ministry found it necessary to modify the National markings of all British aircraft in the light of combat experience to make

Heading: Hurricane Mk I, P2764 US·P of 56 Sqn based at North Weald circa May 1940, in standard Dark Earth/Dark Green uppersurfaces in the B Scheme pattern with Night/White/Aluminium undersides.

Left: Gloster-built Hurricane Mk I, P2728, showing the fuselage roundels in the pre-war Bright Blue/Bright Red colours contrasting with the Squadron applied duller Red and Blue fin stripes.

Right: Formation of Hurricane Mk Is of 73 Sqn., 67 Wing Advanced Air Striking Force flying over France circa April/May 1940. Note 'French style' rudder stripes and lack of Squadron code letters apart from TP·E.

them more prominent. From November 1939, all British aircraft, including Hurricanes, were to sport Red, White and Blue roundels on the fuselage sides, and all British aircraft except home based Day Fighters and Night Bombers were to have Red, White and Blue roundels under their mainplanes. It was with these markings that the home-based Hurricane squadrons settled down to what became known as the 'Phoney War' in the winter of 1939-1940.

Hurricanes in France

Following the declaration of War, as part of an existing agreement with France, the British Expeditionary Force (BEF) was assembled and despatched across the Channel to take up positions behind the French border with Belgium. The BEF was accompanied by the Air Component of the BEF whose role was to support and protect the British Army. Amongst this force were two Hurricane Squadrons, Nos 85 and 87 which formed 60 Wing.

The RAF also despatched the Advanced Air Striking Force (AASF) whose role was to undertake short range offensive operations using its light bomber squadrons. Two Hurricane squadrons, Nos 1 and 73, which formed 67 Wing, accompanied this force in order to protect the bombers and their bases, and to provide general air defence of British forces in North West France.

The Hurricanes sent to France were finished identically to those aircraft at home, but carried Red, White and Blue roundels in the proportions of 1-3-5 on the Night and White undersurfaces of the mainplanes. From November 1939, as with Hurricanes at home, the fuselage roundels were changed to Red, White and Blue, also in the proportions of 1-3-5.

Photographs taken during a visit by King George VI to Lille-Seclin on 6 December 1939, show the Hurricanes of 85 and 87 Sqns to be marked with this revised fuselage roundel, as well as with their Squadron markings. The photographs clearly show that 85 Sqn carried its hexagon marking on the fin in White in addition to its two letter squadron code of VY. It is thought that A Flight carried the hexagon with the 'points' top and bottom, whilst B Flight carried the hexagon with the 'flat faces' top and bottom. Besides their two letter codes of LK, 87 Sqn also appears to have carried its squadron badge inside a standard White spearhead marking on the fin of the aircraft.

Besides the changes to the National markings described above, the Hurricanes of 67 Wing, Nos 1 and 73

Right: Unidentified Hurricane Mk I coded VY·C of 85 Sqn in France circa May/June 1940 showing the unit applied Yellow outer ring to the fuselage roundel re-introduced in early May, and the Red/White/Blue fin stripes on Hurricane VY·E in the background.

Sqns, modified their markings quite considerably by painting out the two letter squadron codes, leaving only the individual aircraft letter; and applying Red, White and Blue stripes to the rudder in the French manner, but with Red leading. This was done to assist the French in identifying the Hurricanes as 'friendly' aircraft.

A significant change is thought to have started to take place in the colour of the undersurfaces of Hurricanes based in France from about January 1940. In his book 'Fighter Pilot', Paul Richey claims that No 1 Sqn was the first RAF squadron to finish the undersurfaces of its aircraft in "duck egg blue". At this same time, several Blenheim bombers were recorded as being finished in a new undersurface shade, possibly the forerunner of the colour Sky. It is difficult to say whether this is true or not, as much depends on what is considered to be 'duck egg blue'. It is however thought that the Hurricanes in France did have what might be described as a 'light blue' shade of paint applied early in 1940. At the time of writing it is difficult to suggest exactly what colour this paint might have been.

Perhaps the best evidence available lies in 'The Battle for Britain - RAF: May to December 1940' by Paul Lucas. Here the author includes two colour photographs which show an unidentified light blue colour on the undersurfaces of Hurricane P2728 delivered in March 1940. This aircraft was originally intended for despatch to France, a fact recorded on its Movement Card. For some reason however, it was not sent to France and was ultimately lost whilst serving with 607 Sqn in September 1940. Other alternatives for the light blue colour might be Sky Blue, or perhaps even a French manufactured paint?

Two other markings changes were made to all RAF aircraft prior to the end of the 'Phoney War'. In early May 1940, instructions were passed to all concerned that a Yellow outer ring was to be re-introduced to the fuselage roundels. The new ring was to be the same width as the existing rings thus giving a roundel of 1-3-5-7 proportions. Whilst this could easily be marked on new production aircraft, it was, in some cases, more difficult to apply to aircraft already in service either because of the presence of existing markings, such as code letters, or because there was not enough room on the fuselage.

Many photographs show where the new Yellow ring was painted around the existing code letter markings, making it appear that the code letters were applied *over the top* of the roundels. Occasionally, where there was not enough room for the new Yellow ring to be applied to the same width as the existing rings, a much narrower Yellow ring was applied instead.

The second change concerned the addition of Red, White and Blue stripes to the fin. 67 Wing had apparently found the rudder stripes applied to their aircraft to be a highly effective identification marking, and as a result a similar marking was ordered to be applied to all RAF aircraft. Because of fears that the application of further coats of paint to the rudder might upset the balance, the new marking was to be applied to the fin. Because the instructions to apply the marking did not specify the size of the

Left: A 46 Sqn Hurricane being hoisted aboard *HMS Glorious* in May 1940, still in its Dark Earth/Dark Green/Night/White scheme, prior to having the 'controversial' Sky Grey fuselage/fin sides applied.

stripes, other than to say they should be of equal width, many different variations were applied. Some Hurricanes had markings which covered the entire fin area, with the White and Blue stripes being of equal width and the Red covering the remaining forward part of the fin; whilst others had equal width stripes which extended to the full height of the fin. The size of the 'fin flash' was finally standardised in August 1940, at 27 inches high by 24 inches wide with each stripe being 8 inches wide.

Hurricanes in Norway

Whilst it is known that the new fuselage roundels and fin markings had been applied to the Hurricanes of 46 Squadron before they were despatched to Norway aboard *HMS Glorious* on 9 May 1940; it is not known with any degree of certainty what colour scheme was carried by these Hurricanes when actually operating in Norway.

Photographs show that at the time they were loaded aboard *HMS Glorious* in the UK, they were finished in the usual Temperate Land Scheme of Dark Earth and Dark Green uppersurfaces, with Night and White undersurfaces. However, there is the possibility that the undersurface colours were altered at some time thereafter. The Night and White recognition markings are said to have been retained under the mainplanes, presumably with Red, White and Blue roundels; but the engine cowling, rear fuselage and tailplanes are thought to have been repainted in Sky Grey. Furthermore, this colour is also thought to have been extended up the fuselage sides and over the fin whilst still retaining the Squadron code letters and 1-3-5-7 roundel and fin flash. Whether the serial number was overpainted is unknown.

No 46 Squadron left Norway by flying their aircraft, (unmodified for carrier deck landings), back aboard *HMS Glorious* on 7 June. Tragically, most of the pilots of the ten remaining aircraft that had been flown aboard, were lost at sea when the ship was sunk by the German battle cruiser *Scharnhorst*, in company with the *Gneisenau*, whilst in transit back to the UK. It is therefore unlikely that this scheme's existence will ever be confirmed.

Dunkirk

Meanwhile, back in the UK, the Dunkirk evacuation was in progress, and in early June, the roundel under the port Night mainplane of Day Fighters operating over the Channel or the French mainland, was modified by the addition of a Yellow outer ring. This was to be "of convenient width, not less than a quarter, or greater than the full width, of the Blue ring". However, no sooner had this additional marking been applied, than the entire undersurfaces were required to be finished in a completely different colour.

The Battle of Britain

With the Battle of France over and the Battle of Britain about to begin, technological advances within Britain's air defence network had rendered the Night and White underside identification marking obsolete. Therefore in early June, this requirement was dropped and a new colour called Sky was introduced. This new pale grey-green colour was to be applied to the undersurfaces of Day Fighters, without any under wing roundels. However, because adequate supplies of this new colour did not exist, several alternative colours appear to have been used instead. The colours used in its place would appear to be Sky Blue BS 381 (1930) No.1; Eau de Nil BS 381 (1930) No. 16; and Sky Grey.

So, when the Battle of Britain started in earnest during July, Hurricanes were camouflaged on their upper surfaces in the Temperate Land Scheme of Dark Earth and Dark Green in either the 'A' or 'B' scheme, with one of the substitutes for Sky, (or as supplies of the proper colour improved, Sky itself), on the undersurfaces, with Red and Blue roundels on top of the mainplanes; Red, White, Blue and Yellow roundels on the fuselage, and Red, White and Blue stripes on the fin. Squadron codes were still applied in Medium Sea Grey, and the serial number remained in Night.

It would appear that whatever colour was used on the undersurfaces of Hurricanes at this time, it was fairly effective as a camouflage. However not having any National markings at all made identification difficult in the middle of a dogfight. This led to the re-introduction of Red, White and Blue roundels on undersurfaces of Day Fighters from the middle of August. It would also appear that Sky eventually started to become the most common undersurface colour on new-build aircraft from September onwards.

Faced with mounting heavy casualties to its bomber force in daylight, during October 1940 the *Luftwaffe* changed its tactics and began employing fighter-bombers at high altitude in daylight, whilst its bomber force operated more and more by night. These changes led to the RAF having to modify the camouflage and markings schemes applied to Hurricanes once again!

Because of the difficulties experienced by the RAF in tracking the high altitude fighter-bombers raids, it once again became necessary to make the identification markings carried by RAF fighters more prominent. This led to the port wing being painted with Special Night distemper which had a Red, White, Blue and Yellow roundel on it. This marking remained in use until April 1941. The other identification markings which were introduced at this time were an 18 inch

Right: Hurricane Mk I, N2359 YB·J of 17 Sqn., based at Debden in June 1940. The undersurfaces were probably painted in one of the Sky substitute colours - possibly Eau de Nil BS 381 (1930) No 16, as was the light coloured spinner. Note the relatively uncommon artwork - a flying Popeye - beneath the cockpit.

Right: A trio of Hurricane Mk Is of 257 Sqn., wearing standard late 1940 style markings. Note the Sky Blue spinners and rear fuselage bands, applied at unit level from November 1940, together with the Special Night port underwing with Yellow outlined roundels. S/Ldr Stanford-Tuck is in the lead aircraft, V6962 DT·A, (sporting a red spinner tip), with P/O Pniak in V7137 DT·G and Sgt Barnes in V6873 DT·O.

wide tail band which was applied just in front of the tailplane, and a coloured spinner. Both of these markings were *supposed* to be applied in Sky, however it would appear that in many cases Sky Blue was used instead.

It is not clear at what point Sky began to be used for these markings, as at this time, both the spinner and tail band markings were not applied on the production line but at Maintenance Units after delivery to the RAF. It is thought that these markings began to be applied on the production line during the summer of 1941, possibly at the same time as the uppersurface camouflage for Day Fighters was revised. These markings then remained in use on Hurricanes for the rest of the war applied in the correct Sky colour.

Night Fighter Hurricanes

When the *Luftwaffe's* medium bomber force switched to night bombing, the RAF was caught without any suitable specialised Night Fighter with which to combat the threat. As an interim solution, several Hurricane squadrons were switched from the Day Fighter role to the Night Fighter role, because of all the single seat Day Fighters in Fighter Command, only the Hurricane was considered suitable for night fighting, not least due in part to its wide track undercarriage.

Up to the middle of November 1940, Night Fighters were finished identically to Day Fighters, but from that point onwards, Night Fighters were to be finished in Special Night overall and marked in the same way as Night Bombers. Thus Red and Blue roundels continued to be applied to the uppersurfaces of the mainplanes whilst Red, White, Blue and Yellow roundels in the proportion of 1-3-5-7 were applied to the fuselage. The fins now carried the 27 inch high by 24 inch wide flash as standard. Squadron codes were still applied in Medium Sea Grey as was the 8 inch high serial number, originally, but this was later changed to Red to conform with the finish of Night Bombers. Underwing roundels were also applied for a short time before being abandoned. Hurricanes continued to use this scheme until 1942.

A change in camouflage

By the spring of 1941, changes in Hurricane camouflage were afoot. The first concerned the production painting of the aircraft. By this stage, it was seen as a drain on resources to continue with the alternative 'A' and 'B' schemes. Therefore in the spring of 1941, a rationalisation of camouflage schemes was carried out across the aircraft industry with the result that all Hurricane's manufacturers, including Hawkers, had to settle on just one of the two schemes. Hawkers settled on the 'A' Scheme as did most of the others, and thereafter virtually every Hurricane built had the same disruptive pattern on the upper surfaces.

The second change, which was one of colour, came about due to an operational requirement. As a result of meeting the *Luftwaffe* at greater altitudes during the closing phase of the Battle of Britain, the RAF found that the Temperate Land Scheme of Dark Earth and Dark Green was inferior to the 'new' grey camouflage colours being introduced by the *Luftwaffe* fighters operating at those altitudes. As a result, work was put in hand at the RAE at Farnborough and Air Fighting Development Unit (AFDU) at Duxford to try to find a compromise colour scheme which would be suitable for Day Fighters at greater altitudes as well as providing some measure of protection when the aircraft was parked on an airfield.

After initial trials at the AFDU, the service trials were carried out by the Hurricanes of 56 Sqn. Eventually, by August 1941, the colours decided upon were Dark Green and a new colour called Ocean Grey on the uppersurfaces; with Medium Sea Grey on the undersurfaces. Again due to initial shortages of the new Ocean Grey paint, squadrons were advised to mix their own grey colour by mixing seven parts Medium Sea Grey to one part Night. The resulting shade was not an exact match for Ocean Grey, and was known colloquially as 'mixed grey'. It is almost impossible to say exactly what this colour would have looked like since every mix could have been slightly different.

At the same time as the new camouflage scheme was introduced, the colour of the squadron code letters was changed to Sky, and a further recognition marking was added in the form of Yellow leading edge stripes on the mainplane s, from approximately mid-way along the wing out to the extreme wing tip. The National markings and the serial number remained unchanged.

When the new scheme became established in production, it was officially named the Day Fighter Scheme and remained in use for the rest of World War Two, and in the event, beyond.

Russian excursion

At the same time that these changes were being put into effect, two squadrons equipped with the Hurricane Mk IIa and Mk IIb, were despatched around the North Cape to the Soviet Union. Following the German attack in June 1941, Britain had pledged to help the Soviets, and this had taken the form of sending military supplies to the North Russian ports of Archangel and Murmansk. Part of these supplies were the Hurricane IIs, some of which were fitted with tropical filters as they had originally been intended for delivery to the Middle East.

The two Squadrons, 81 and 134, which made up 151 Wing, had two roles to fulfill. Firstly they were to provide air defence for the ports, which not surprisingly had become major targets for the *Luftwaffe*; and secondly to train Soviet pilots to fly the Hurricanes which were due to be supplied to them.

The Hurricanes flown by 151 Wing appear to have been finished in the Temperate Land Scheme of Dark Earth and Dark Green on their uppersurfaces with what is thought to have been Sky Blue undersurfaces, as despite the changes in camouflage which were going on at squadron level in the UK, the new Day Fighter Scheme was not yet established on the production line. The usual RAF National markings were carried in the usual places with Sky Blue

Left: Hurricane Mk I, P2798 LK·A of 87 Sqn - the same aeroplane as featured on the contents page - overpainted in Special Night overall for the Night Fighter role.

Right: Hurricane Mk II, Z5227 FE·53 of 81 Sqn., 151 Wing at Vaenga, Russia, in the autumn of 1941 and still in the Temperate Land Scheme of Dark Earth and Dark Green uppersurfaces probably with Sky Blue undersides, despite the introduction of the new Day Fighter Scheme in August.

spinners. The tail band was omitted, which might be a further indication that even at this date, these markings were still being applied at MUs rather than on the production line.

The squadron markings were also somewhat unusual. In theory 81 Sqn's Hurricanes should have been coded FV whilst those of 134 Sqn should have been GV. What actually happened was that both squadrons used only the first letter of their allocation; thus 81 Sqn was coded F and 134 Sqn was coded G. The individual aircraft identification letter was then applied directly next to the squadron letter thus producing what appeared to be a two letter code, for example GO (Z5236) or FE (Z5277). These markings appear to have been painted onto the Hurricanes in front of the roundel on both sides of the fuselage. The space behind the roundel was used to apply a two digit numeral in a slightly eastern European 'cyrillic-style', presumably in line with Soviet VVS practice. These fuselage markings appear to have been applied in various combinations of grey and white, with the RAF code letters (presumably) in standard Medium Sea Grey, and the cyrillic-style numbers in either pale grey and/or white. 151 Wing successfully carried out its duties in the Soviet Union and by the end of November had handed over its remaining aircraft to the Soviets and sailed home.

Changes in National markings

Late 1941 found the RAF examining the National markings carried by its aircraft once again. The original stimulus for this had come from Bomber Command whose experiences of having aircraft coned in searchlights over Germany had led to requests for changes to be made. At the same time there was also some concern that the roundels were perhaps just a little too prominent in daylight as well.

As a result, it was decided to review the whole subject of roundels and fin markings with the aim of devising new markings which whilst remaining distinctive enough for identification purposes, were not more conspicuous than the aircraft which carried them. In meeting this aim, no change was to be made in the colours used, or the general form of the markings.

A suggestion was put forward that the best way of reducing visibility by day would be to reduce the size of the white and yellow rings, on the fuselage and/or underwing roundels, and after various trials, this is what was done. The new fuselage roundel style had ring widths in the proportions of Red 6, White 1, Blue 4

Right: Hurricane Mk IIc, BD936 ZY·S of 247 Sqn., finished in overall Special Night for Intruder operations and sporting the new National markings initially adopted for Night Fighters in January 1942.

and Yellow 1, with the underwing roundel consisting of the same proportions but without the outer Yellow ring.

When a fuselage roundel with a diameter of 4 ft to this design was tested on a dull day it was found to be visible for up to a quarter of a mile, thus being only about half as visible as the 1-3-5-7 proportion roundel then currently in use. The roundel effect of the separate colour bands was visible at about a third of a mile - about the same distance as the roundel currently in use.

It was recommended that the new fuselage roundels be restricted to three sizes - 18 inch diameter for small aircraft; 36 inch diameter for medium aircraft; and 54 inch diameter for large aircraft.

Modifications to the fin flash were also considered, with alterations to the then standard 27 inch high by 24 inch wide marking being carried out. The new fin flash had a reduced 2 inch wide band of White separating 11 inch wide bands of Red and Blue. This was found to have a visibility about equal to that of the new roundel.

Similarly to the roundel, it was recommended that the new fin flash be restricted to three sizes for small, medium and large aircraft. The width of the White band was to remain at 2 inches for all three sizes, with the flash being 18 inches square for small aircraft; 24 inches square for medium size aircraft; and 36 inches square for large aircraft.

These proposed changes to the fuselage/underwing roundels and fin flashes were duly submitted to the Air Ministry, and by the end of January 1942, Fighter Command had been instructed to adopt the new markings, initially for its Night Fighters.

By January 1942, the Hurricane had been superseded as a Night fighter by such specialised types as the Beaufighter and Mosquito which were equipped with Airborne Interception (AI) radar. Despite this, the Hurricane continued to be used as an Intruder in the overall Special Night finish described earlier. Photographs of the period would

suggest that at least one Hurricane Intruder squadron, No 247, applied the new fuselage roundel to their aircraft in a small size which had an outside diameter of approximately 18 inches. The fin flash also appears to have been smaller than usual, thought to be approximately 18 inches square. This bestowed the aircraft with a very unusual appearance which was increased by the squadron code and individual aircraft letters all being located to the rear of the fuselage roundel and separated by a hyphen. Whilst they remained Red in colour, like the fuselage roundel and fin flash, they too were of a much smaller size than usual.

Large scale trials of the new markings for other roles were authorised, and having been considered successful by the end of April 1942, the introduction of the new type of underwing and fuselage roundels and fin flashes for all British types of aircraft was authorised. At the same time, all the markings were given official titles. 'National marking I' was the title of the Red and Blue roundel applied to the upper surfaces of the mainplanes; 'National marking II' was the title of the Red, White and Blue roundel applied to the under surfaces of the mainplanes; and 'National marking III' was the title given to the Red, White, Blue and Yellow roundel applied to the sides of the fuselage. The fin flash was titled 'Fin marking (i)'. For single seat fighters, such as the Hurricane, the size of the roundels and fin flashes were those specified for medium size aircraft, ie 32 inch National marking II under the mainplanes, and 36 inch National marking III on the fuselage sides. Fin marking (i) was to be 24 inch square. The underwing and fuselage roundels and fin flashes remained in use on European-based Hurricanes until the end of the war without further modification. The Red and Blue upperwing roundel, (National marking I), continued to vary in size amongst all RAF-operated aeroplanes, invariably depending upon the available chord from the leading edge to the aileron hinge line,

Right: Hurricane Mk IIc of 1 Sqn., in the Day Fighter Scheme consisting of what appears to be Mixed Grey and Dark Green uppersurfaces, with the then new fuselage and fin National markings, Sky spinner, tail band and Squadron codes.

and on the Hurricane was generally 49 inches in diameter.

Intruder scheme

During August 1942 the camouflage applied to the RAF's Night Fighters was completely changed, and therefore by proxy, so was the camouflage applied to the Intruder Hurricanes. Special Night was originally adopted for Night Fighters because it was thought that Special Night offered protection from searchlights, and therefore made it an ideal colour for Night Fighters. Subsequent experience showed how wrong this idea was. The problem of camouflaging a Night Fighter was primarily one of tonal values. When observed in flight, the fighter appeared as a solid dark object against a lighter background which varied in tone depending on the direction of approach taken. Therefore if the fighter was painted black, the contrast between it and any background was intensified and the fighter would become visible at a much greater range than if the contrast were reduced.

Trials with various schemes of green and grey took place throughout 1941 and into 1942 before Fighter Command concluded that the uppersurfaces of Night Fighters should be camouflaged in a similar way to those of Day Fighters, only they should be a little bit lighter in tone. Therefore in August 1942, Fighter Command re-defined the finish it wished to be applied to its Night Fighters.

These aircraft were to be finished Medium Sea Grey overall, with a Dark Green disruptive pattern, ostensibly to the 'A' Scheme. However, this finish did not apply to Intruders at first. For some reason, when details of the Intruder Scheme were initially promulgated in October 1942, the uppersurfaces were given as those of the Day Fighter Scheme, ie Dark Green and Ocean Grey, and because Intruder Hurricanes might be subjected to searchlights over enemy territory, they were allowed to retain their Special Night undersurfaces. As Hurricanes were being produced with the Day Fighter Scheme on the uppersurfaces as a matter of course, it would only necessitate the undersurfaces being repainted in Special Night to give the new scheme.

No 87 Squadron is thought to have operated over Dieppe on 19 August 1942 in this scheme. The colour of the squadron codes on 87 Squadron's aircraft is uncertain, but was probably Sky or possibly even Sky Grey.

December 1942 saw the official promulgation of the Intruder Scheme proper, which consisted of the Night Fighter Scheme on the uppersurfaces, (ie Medium Sea Grey with a Dark Green disruptive pattern), and still with Special Night on the undersurfaces. The National markings on the uppersurfaces of the wings were to remain the Red and Blue roundel (National marking I), whilst those on the fuselage were to be the newly proportioned Red, White, Blue and Yellow roundel (National marking III). The new style fin flashes (Fin marking (i)) were retained. No roundels were to be carried under the mainplanes. Both the fuselage serial number and the squadron codes were to be Red.

The only further modification made to the Intruder Scheme for the rest of the war was the replacement of Special Night with Night from December 1942 onwards.

Fighter-bomber role

As the Hurricane came to be outclassed as a fighter from 1942 onwards, it became a successful Fighter-bomber carrying a variety of offensive stores from 250lb to 500lb bombs, through 40mm cannons, to 60lb rocket projectiles. All of

Right: Formation shot of No 87 Sqn Hurricane IIbs and IIcs, with the newly introduced National marking III on their fuselage sides and Fin marking (i), in a unit-applied Intruder Scheme of either Medium Sea Grey, Mixed Grey or Ocean Grey, and Dark Green uppersurfaces with Special Night undersides.

Left: 40mm gun-armed Hurricane Mk IId, KX413 FJ·M of 164 Sqn., engaged on anti-shipping operations from Middle Wallop in the summer of 1943, in the standard Day Fighter Scheme and markings.

these Fighter-bombers left the production line and served in the Day Fighter Scheme of Ocean Grey and Dark Green uppersurfaces with Medium Sea Grey undersurfaces to the end of the war.

The Hurricane was also extensively used between 1942 and 1945 for various second line duties such as Meteorological Reconnaissance, Radar Calibration, Bomber Defence Training, Operational Training, and Communications Duties. For the vast majority of these duties, the Hurricanes retained the normal Day Fighter Scheme.

With the launching of 'Operation Overlord' in June 1944, the requirement arose for a fast courier service between the UK and the Continent which was filled by the creation of the Air Despatch Letter Flight which was expanded into the Air Despatch Letter Service (ADLS) Squadron at Northolt in December 1944. Amongst other types, this unit used a number of Hurricanes finished in the Day Fighter Scheme, coded DR with the letters ADLS stencilled under the canopy which received the black and white AAEF invasion stripes. In the months following the invasion, in common with other tactical aircraft, the stripes were restricted to the undersurfaces of the wings and rear fuselage.

Final roundel changes

In January 1945, the National marking on the uppersurfaces of the wings was modified, as an aid to the identification of RAF aircraft for those aircraft of Allied nations operating alongside the RAF. This apparently came about as a result of continuing problems experienced with aircraft identification in daylight following the Normandy landings. It was therefore decided to introduce a Red, White and Blue roundel on the wing uppersurfaces in place of the Red and Blue style.

From 7 January, all aircraft other than those whose primary role was night operations, and aircraft operating in Air Command South East Asia and the Pacific, were to revert to Red, White and Blue roundels on the upper surfaces of the mainplanes in place of National marking I. The new marking was designated National marking IA and this remained in service until the end of the war - and beyond.

Balkan Air Force

The spring of 1945 found the Hurricane still in front line service in the Balkan Air Force, operating over Yugoslavia in support of Tito's partisans with Nos 6 and 351 Squadrons who were flying the bomb and rocket-armed Hurricane Mk IV.

At this time, the Air Ministry in London was in the process of conducting a survey of all the Operational Commands to try and find out whether it would be possible to abandon the use of camouflage on some types of aircraft altogether. In April 1945, HQ Balkan Air Force wrote to HQ Mediterranean Allied Air Forces stating that they required all replacement Beaufighters, Spitfires, Mustangs and Hurricanes to be camouflaged, because all these aircraft were engaged in low flying attacks in mountainous country where the concealment afforded by camouflage was necessary to give an element of surprise. A similar view was held by Headquarters RAF Middle East who considered that camouflage for Day Fighters was not necessary, but was desirable for low level attack aircraft.

At this time the aircraft of both 6 and 351 squadrons were finished in the Day Fighter Scheme of Ocean Grey and Dark Green on the uppersurfaces, with what is thought to be Medium Sea Grey on the undersurfaces. However, there is some doubt about the actual undersurface colour because it was not unknown for colours such as Sky Blue, Azure Blue, or Light Mediterranean Blue to be applied to the undersurfaces of day flying aircraft in the Mediterranean Theatre, even this late on in the war.

No 6 Squadron carried the usual national markings in the usual places including the new Red, White and Blue National marking IA on the uppersurfaces of the wings and the standard Sky spinner and tail band markings with Yellow wing leading edges on the mainplanes. No squadron codes were carried, the Hurricanes just being marked with an individual aircraft letter behind the roundel - in either Sky or Sky Blue.

The aircraft of the Yugoslav-manned 351 squadron carried 'Yugoslav-style' national markings. These consisted of a red star superimposed on a modified National marking IA on the uppersurface of the mainplanes; a red star superimposed on a modified National marking II on the undersurface of the mainplanes; a red star superimposed on a modified National marking III on the fuselage, and a red star superimposed on the white band of a modified Fin marking (i) in which the bands were all of equal size with the blue band leading.

Having seen front-line service throughout the World War Two, the Hurricane continued to serve into peacetime, as No 6 Sqn kept is Hurricanes until January 1947, by which time they were finished in the post-war scheme of overall painted Aluminium.

Right: Hurricane Mk IVs of 351 (Yugoslav) Sqn., Balkan Air Force, being armed with 60lb Rocket Projectiles. The aircraft were finished in the Day Fighter Scheme of Ocean Grey and Dark Green uppersurfaces, but *may* have had a shade of 'light blue' on the undersurfaces. Note the modified National markings with superimposed red stars applied.

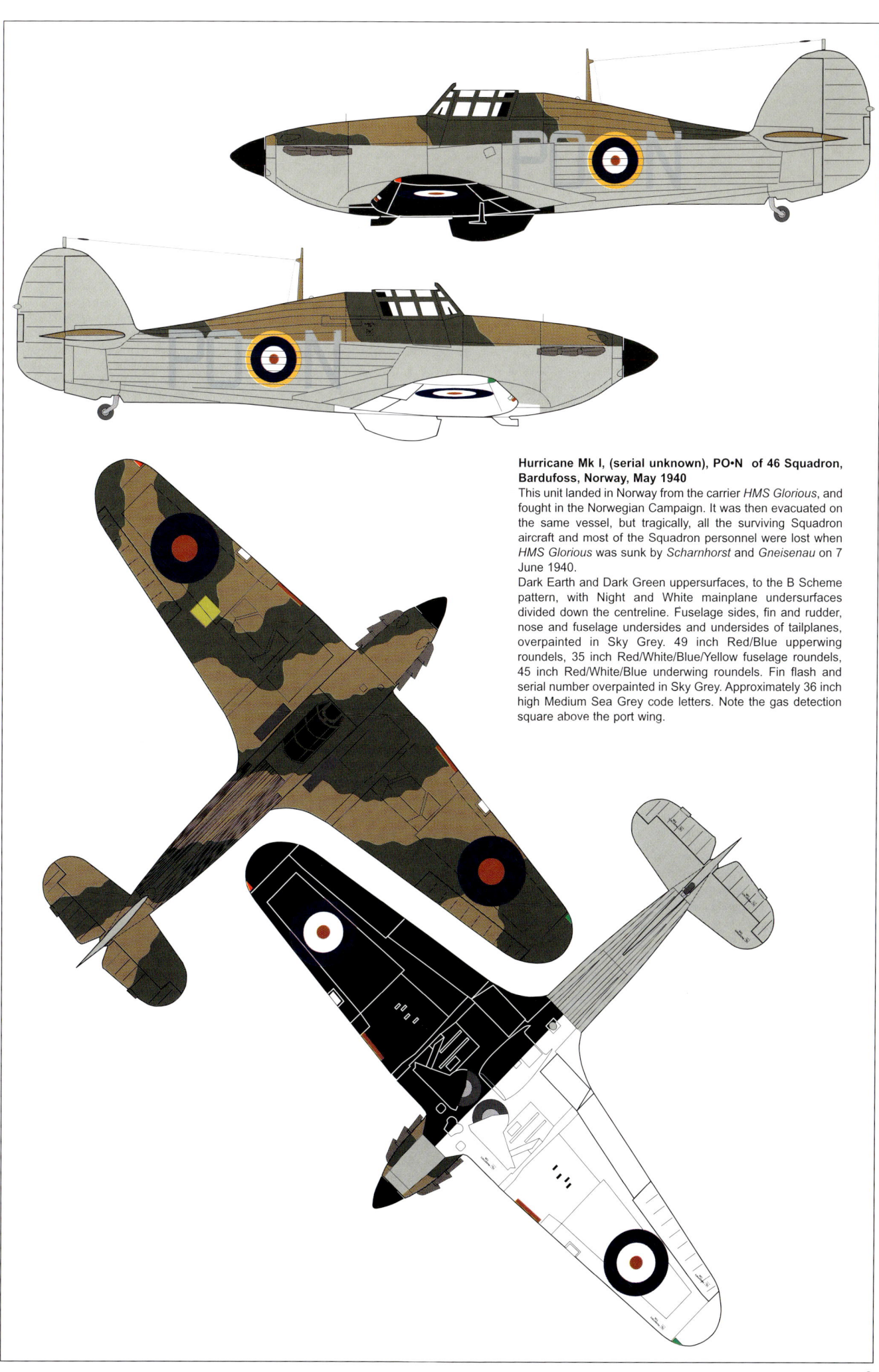

Hurricane Mk I, (serial unknown), PO•N of 46 Squadron, Bardufoss, Norway, May 1940

This unit landed in Norway from the carrier *HMS Glorious*, and fought in the Norwegian Campaign. It was then evacuated on the same vessel, but tragically, all the surviving Squadron aircraft and most of the Squadron personnel were lost when *HMS Glorious* was sunk by *Scharnhorst* and *Gneisenau* on 7 June 1940.

Dark Earth and Dark Green uppersurfaces, to the B Scheme pattern, with Night and White mainplane undersurfaces divided down the centreline. Fuselage sides, fin and rudder, nose and fuselage undersides and undersides of tailplanes, overpainted in Sky Grey. 49 inch Red/Blue upperwing roundels, 35 inch Red/White/Blue/Yellow fuselage roundels, 45 inch Red/White/Blue underwing roundels. Fin flash and serial number overpainted in Sky Grey. Approximately 36 inch high Medium Sea Grey code letters. Note the gas detection square above the port wing.

Hurricane Mk I, (serial unknown), GG•L of 151 Squadron, Sealand, mid-1939
Dark Earth and Dark Green uppersurfaces, to the A Scheme pattern, with Night and White undersurfaces divided centrally down the fuselage centreline. 35 inch Red/Blue upperwing roundels, (converted from the factory applied 49 inch Red/White/Blue/Yellow style with the Yellow overpainted and the Red and Blue increased to cover the White area), and 25 inch fuselage roundels similarly modified from the original Red/White/Blue/Yellow style. No underwing roundels were carried, and the serial number had been overpainted. The 36 inch high Medium Sea Grey Squadron codes were in the pre-war allocation. Note the squadron badge spearhead on the fin.

Hurricane Mk I, (serial unknown), RO•P of 29 Squadron, Debden, September 1939
Dark Earth and Dark Green uppersurfaces, to the B Scheme pattern, with Night and White undersurfaces divided centrally down the fuselage centreline. 35 inch Red/Blue upperwing roundels, (converted from the factory applied 49 inch Red/White/Blue/Yellow style with the Yellow overpainted and the Red and Blue increased to cover the White area), and 35 inch fuselage roundels modified from the original Red/White/Blue/Yellow style, but this time by overpainting the Yellow and White areas by increasing the Red and Blue areas. No underwing roundels were carried, and the serial number had been overpainted. The pre-war allocation Medium Sea Grey Squadron codes were approximately 27 inches high and of a thinner stroke to the aircraft above.

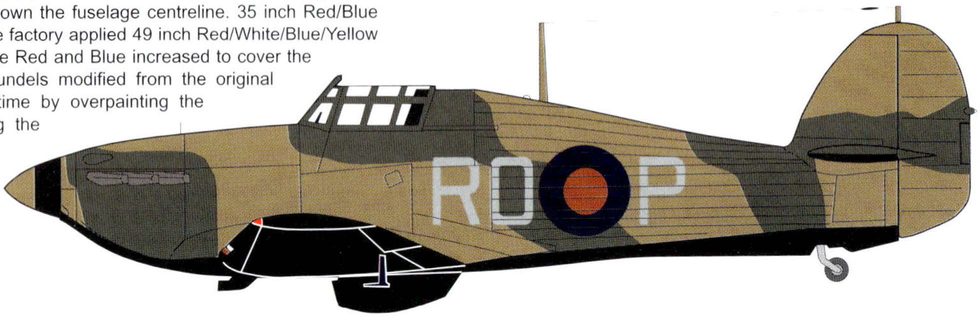

Hurricane Mk I, L1909, LR•R of 56 Squadron, RAF North Weald, mid-1939
Dark Earth and Dark Green uppersurfaces, to the B Scheme pattern, with Night and White mainplane undersurfaces divided centrally down the centreline and Aluminium nose, rear fuselage and tailplane undersides. 35 inch Red/Blue upperwing roundels, (converted from the factory applied 49 inch Red/White/Blue/Yellow style with the Yellow overpainted and the Red and Blue increased to cover the White area), and 25 inch fuselage roundels similarly modified from the original Red/White/Blue/Yellow style. No underwing roundels were carried. The Medium Sea Grey Squadron codes were approximately 36 inches high and in the pre-war allocation.

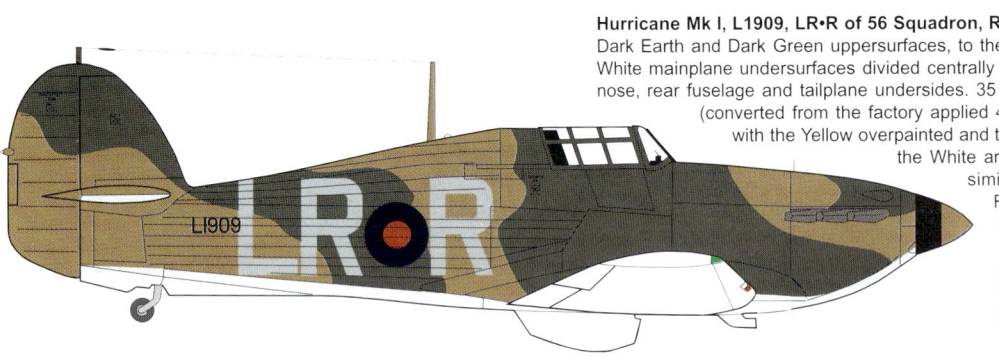

Hurricane Mk I, (serial unknown), NQ•M of 43 Squadron, Tangmere, mid-1939
Dark Earth and Dark Green uppersurfaces, to the A Scheme pattern, with Night and White mainplane undersurfaces divided centrally down the centreline and Aluminium nose, rear fuselage and tailplane undersides. 35 inch Red/Blue upperwing roundels, (converted from the factory applied 49 inch Red/White/Blue/Yellow style with the Yellow overpainted and the Red and Blue increased to cover the White area), and 21 inch fuselage roundels modified from the original Red/White/Blue/Yellow style. No underwing roundels were carried and the serial number had been overpainted. The Medium Sea Grey Squadron codes were approximately 30 inches high and in the pre-war allocation.

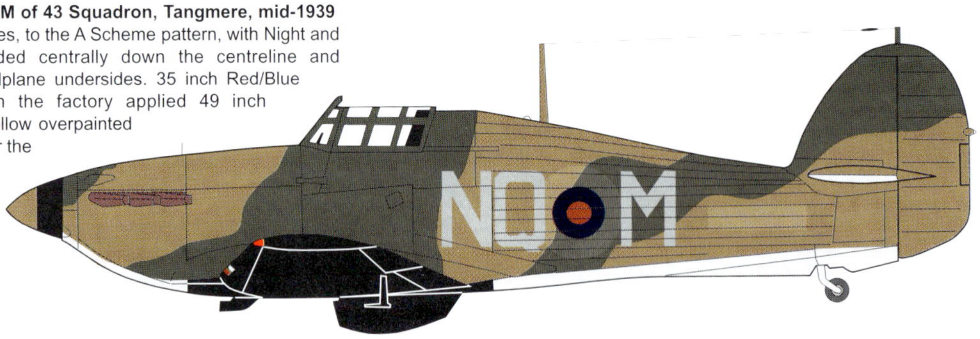

Hurricane Mk I, (serial unknown), JU•B of 111 Squadron, Wick, 1939
Dark Earth and Dark Green uppersurfaces, to the A Scheme pattern, with Night and White undersurfaces divided centrally down the fuselage centreline. 35 inch Red/Blue upperwing roundels, (converted from the factory applied 49 inch Red/White/Blue/Yellow style with the Yellow overpainted and the Red and Blue increased to cover the White area), and 35 inch Red/White/Blue fuselage roundels modified from the original Red/White/Blue/Yellow style, but this time by just overpainting the Yellow outer ring. No underwing roundels were carried, and the serial number had again been overpainted. The wartime allocation Medium Sea Grey Squadron codes were approximately 24 inches high and of a thinner stroke to some of the aircraft above. At this time, the unit was tasked with the defence of the Home Fleet, based at Scapa Flow.

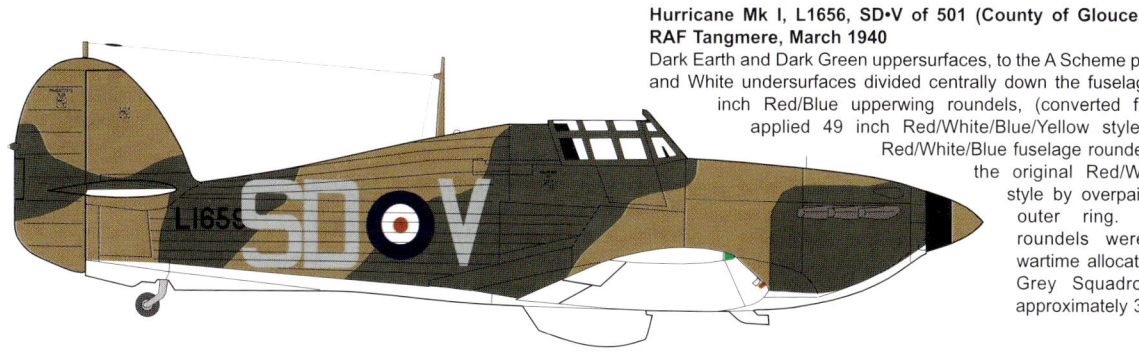

Hurricane Mk I, L1656, SD•V of 501 (County of Gloucester) Squadron, RAF Tangmere, March 1940
Dark Earth and Dark Green uppersurfaces, to the A Scheme pattern, with Night and White undersurfaces divided centrally down the fuselage centreline. 35 inch Red/Blue upperwing roundels, (converted from the factory applied 49 inch Red/White/Blue/Yellow style), and 25 inch Red/White/Blue fuselage roundels modified from the original Red/White/Blue/Yellow style by overpainting the Yellow outer ring. No underwing roundels were carried. The wartime allocation Medium Sea Grey Squadron codes were approximately 33 inches high.

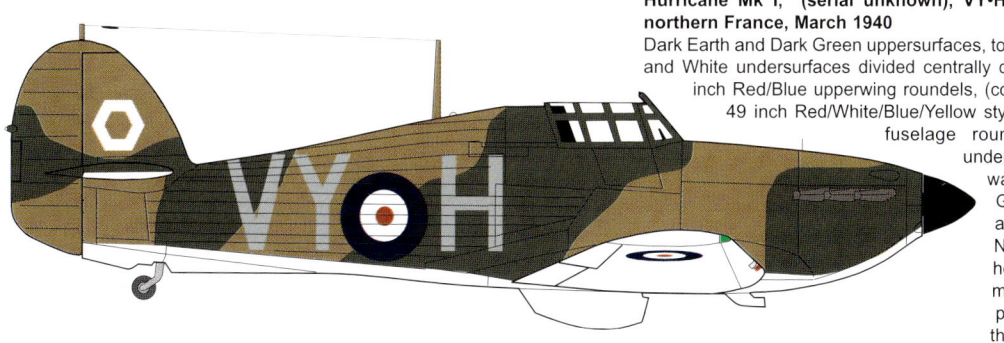

Hurricane Mk I, (serial unknown), VY•H of 85 Squadron, Lille-Seclin, northern France, March 1940
Dark Earth and Dark Green uppersurfaces, to the A Scheme pattern, with Night and White undersurfaces divided centrally down the fuselage centreline. 35 inch Red/Blue upperwing roundels, (converted from the factory applied 49 inch Red/White/Blue/Yellow style), and 35 inch Red/White/Blue fuselage roundels. Approximately 30 inch underwing roundels were carried. The wartime allocation Medium Sea Grey Squadron codes were approximately 36 inches high. Note the Squadron's white hexagon marking on the fin. This machine was still fitted with the pole style radio mast, but had a three-bladed de Havilland propeller.

Hurricane Mk I, (serial unknown), LK•P of 87 Squadron, Lille-Seclin, northern France, March 1940
Dark Earth and Dark Green uppersurfaces, to the B Scheme pattern, with Night and White mainplane undersurfaces divided centrally down the centreline and Aluminium nose, rear fuselage and tailplane undersides. 35 inch Red/Blue upperwing roundels, (converted from the factory applied 49 inch Red/White/Blue/Yellow style), and 25 inch Red/White/Blue fuselage roundels modified from the original Red/White/Blue/Yellow style by overpainting the Yellow outer ring. Approximately 45 inch underwing roundels were carried. The wartime allocation Medium Sea Grey Squadron codes were approximately 30 inches high. This was an early machine, with a pole radio mast and a two-bladed Watts propeller.

Hurricane Mk I, P2545, (TP)•L of 73 Squadron, 67 Wing, Advanced Air Striking Force, (AASF), Rouvres, France, spring 1940
Dark Earth and Dark Green uppersurfaces, to the B Scheme pattern, with Night and White undersurfaces divided centrally down the fuselage centreline. 49 inch Red/Blue upperwing roundels, and 35 inch Red/White/Blue fuselage roundels. Approximately 45 inch underwing roundels were carried. The Medium Sea Grey Squadron codes had been painted out leaving only the individual aircraft letter which was approximately 24 inches high. Note the 67 Wing practice of painting the rudder with French style Red/White/Blue stripes. This machine was fitted with a three-bladed de Havilland propeller.

Hurricane Mk I, P2575, (TP)•J of 73 Squadron, 67 Wing, Advanced Air Striking Force, Rouvres in northern France in March 1940
Dark Earth and Dark Green uppersurfaces, to the A Scheme pattern, with with Night and White mainplane undersurfaces divided centrally down the centreline and Aluminium nose, rear fuselage and tailplane undersides. 49 inch Red/Blue upperwing roundels, and 35 inch Red/White/Blue fuselage roundels. Approximately 45 inch underwing roundels were carried. Like the aircraft above. the Medium Sea Grey Squadron codes had been painted out leaving only the individual aircraft letter which was approximately 30 inches high. Note the 67 Wing practice of painting the rudder with French style Red/White/Blue stripes. This machine was also fitted with a three-bladed de Havilland propeller.

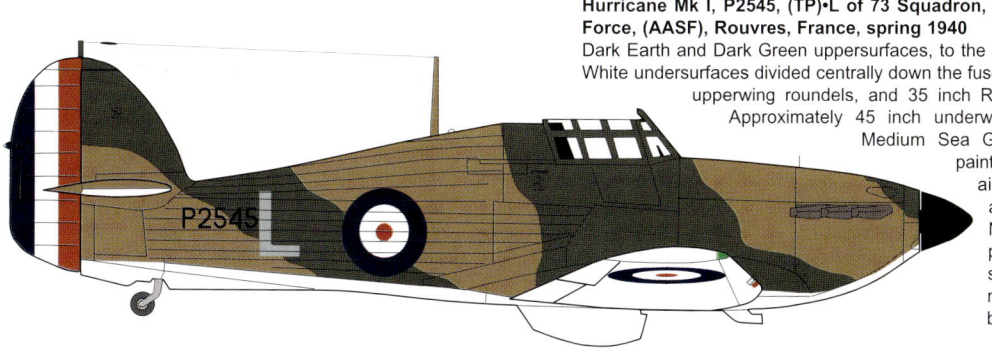

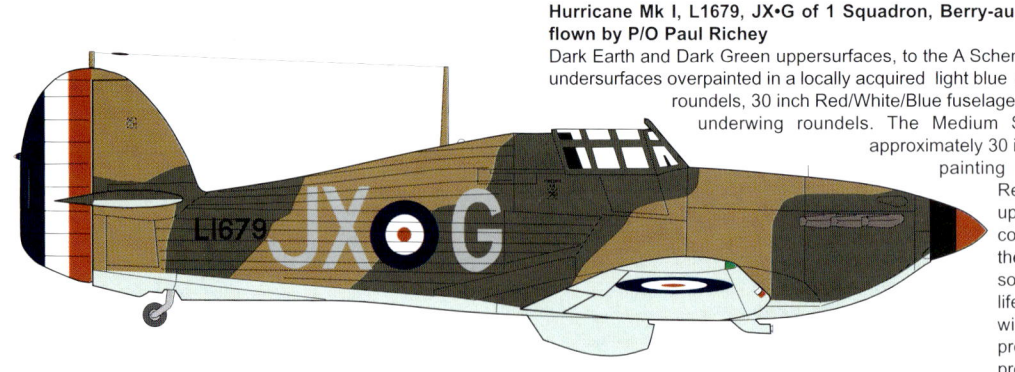

Hurricane Mk I, L1679, JX·G of 1 Squadron, Berry-au-Bac, northern France, May 1940, flown by P/O Paul Richey
Dark Earth and Dark Green uppersurfaces, to the A Scheme pattern, with the Night and White undersurfaces overpainted in a locally acquired light blue shade. 49 inch Red/Blue upperwing roundels, 30 inch Red/White/Blue fuselage roundels and approximately 45 inch underwing roundels. The Medium Sea Grey Squadron codes were approximately 30 inches high. The 67 Wing practice of painting the rudder with French style Red/White/Blue stripes continued right up to the *Blitzkrieg* of 10 May, and contemporary photographs show that the serial number was painted out at some time during the aircraft s service life. This machine has yet to be fitted with a three-bladed de Havilland propeller, and its Watts two-bladed propeller had a Red tip.

Hurricane Mk I, L1774, LK·D of 87 Squadron, Lille-Seclin, France, May 1940
Dark Earth and Dark Green uppersurfaces, to the A Scheme pattern, with the Night and White undersurfaces divided centrally down the fuselage centreline. 49 inch Red/Blue upperwing roundels, 35 inch Red/White/Blue fuselage roundels thinly outlined in Yellow and approximately 45 inch underwing roundels. Approximately 7 inch wide Red/White/Blue fin stripes were applied up the full height of the fin. The Medium Sea Grey Squadron codes were approximately 30 inches high.

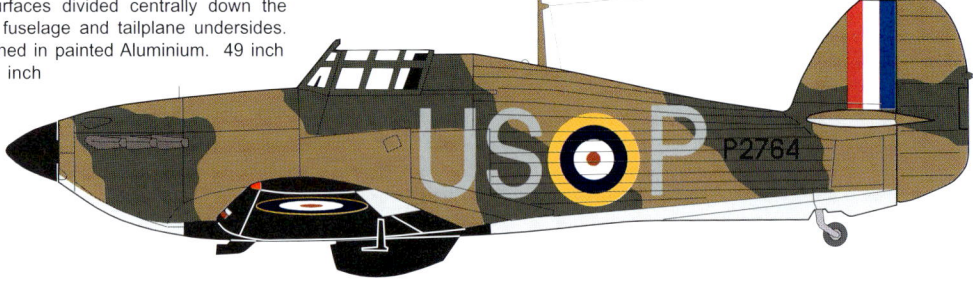

Hurricane Mk I, P2764, US·P of 56 Squadron, North Weald, May 1940
Dark Earth and Dark Green uppersurfaces, to the B Scheme pattern, with Night and White mainplane undersurfaces divided centrally down the centreline and Aluminium nose, rear fuselage and tailplane undersides. Undersurfaces of both ailerons remained in painted Aluminium. 49 inch Red/Blue upperwing roundels, 35 inch Red/White/Blue/Yellow fuselage roundels and approximately 45 inch underwing roundels, the one under the port (Night) wing being thinly outlined in Yellow. Approximately 7 inch wide fin stripes in the pre-war bright colours were applied up the full height of the fin. The Medium Sea Grey Squadron codes were approximately 36 inches high.

Hurricane Mk I, L1754, DZ·E of 151 Squadron, Martlesham Heath, May/June 1940
Dark Earth and Dark Green uppersurfaces, to the A Scheme pattern, with Night and White undersurfaces divided centrally down the centreline. 49 inch Red/Blue upperwing roundels, 35 inch Red/White/Blue/Yellow fuselage roundels with the Yellow outer ring truncated along the upper/under camouflage demarcation line. Approximately 45 inch underwing roundels, the one under the port (Night) wing being thinly outlined in Yellow. Fin flash consisted of 9 inch wide Blue and White stripes with the entire front of the fin in Red. The Medium Sea Grey Squadron codes were approximately 36 inches high.

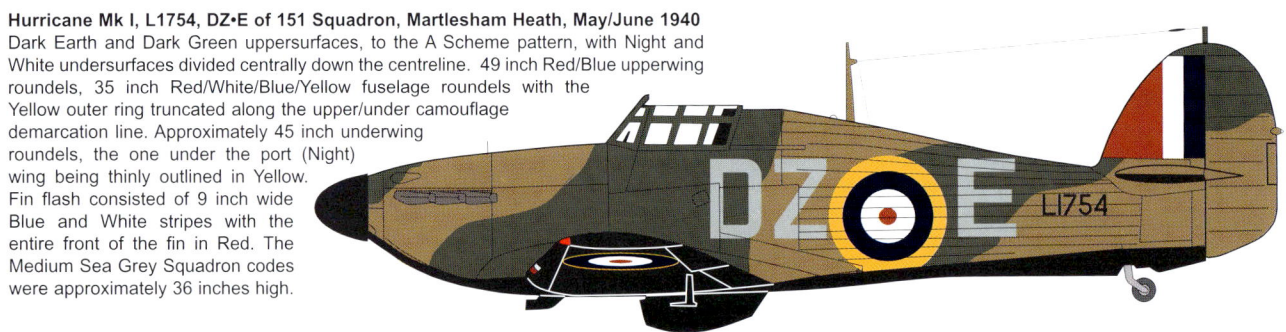

Hurricane Mk I, (serial unknown), SO·E of 145 Squadron, Croydon, June 1940
Dark Earth and Dark Green uppersurfaces, to the A Scheme pattern. Undersurfaces re-painted in one of the Sky substitute colours - possibly the duck egg green shade - Eau de Nil BS 381 (1930) No 16. 49 inch Red/Blue upperwing roundels; non-standard approximately 45 inch Red/White/Blue fuselage roundels with a thin Yellow outer ring truncated along the upper/under camouflage demarcation line. No underwing roundels were carried and the serial number was painted out. Fin flash consisted of three 9 inch wide Red/White/Blue stripes extending the full height of the fin. The Medium Sea Grey Squadron codes were approximately 30 inches high.

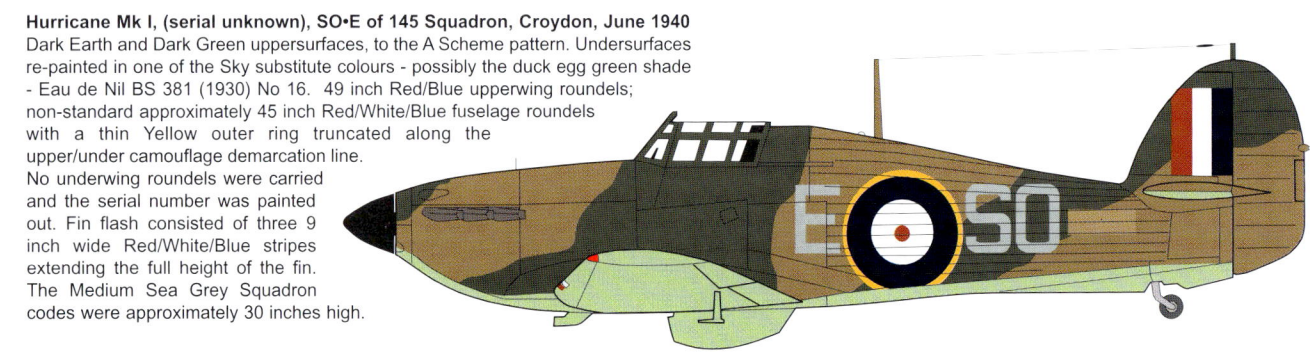

Hurricane Mk I, N2359, YB•J of 17 Squadron, Debden, June 1940
Dark Earth and Dark Green uppersurfaces, to the A Scheme pattern. Undersurfaces re-painted in one of the Sky substitute colours - possibly the duck egg green shade - Eau de Nil BS 381 (1930) No 16. 49 inch Red/Blue upperwing roundels; 49 inch Red/White/Blue fuselage roundels with the Yellow outer ring truncated along the upper/under camouflage demarcation line. No underwing roundels were carried. Fin flash consisted of 9 inch wide Blue and White stripes with the entire front of the fin in Red. The Medium Sea Grey Squadron codes were approximately 30 inches high. Note the duck egg green spinner and winged Popeye cartoon under the cockpit.

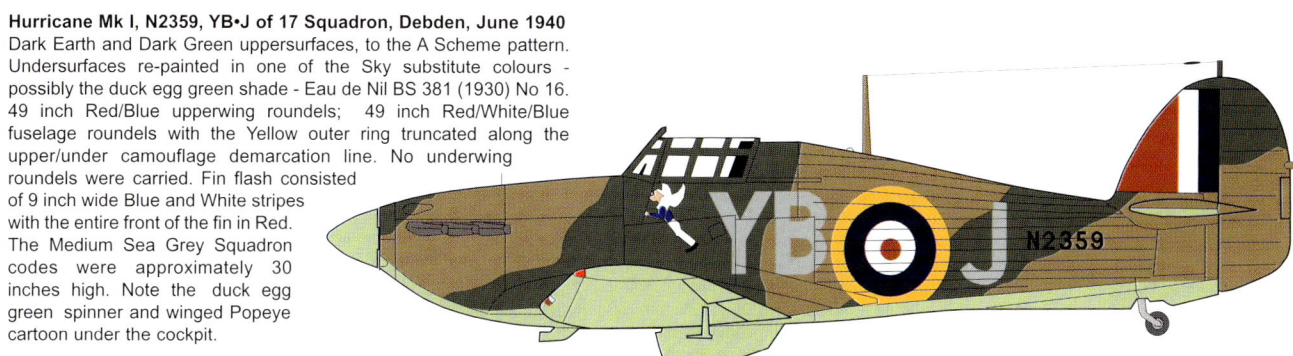

Hurricane Mk I, P2923, VY•R of 85 Squadron, Martlesham Heath, August 1940
Dark Earth and Dark Green uppersurfaces, to the A Scheme pattern. Undersurfaces re-painted in one of the Sky substitute colours - possibly the duck egg blue shade - Sky Blue BS 381 (1930) No 1. 49 inch Red/Blue upperwing roundels; 49 inch Red/White/Blue/Yellow fuselage roundels with the Yellow outer ring truncated along the upper/under camouflage demarcation line. No underwing roundels were carried and the fin flash consisted of 9 inch wide Blue and White stripes with the entire front of the fin in Red. The Medium Sea Grey Squadron codes were approximately 36 inches high. Note the red and white striped spinner and the wavy undersurface paint demarcation on the nose.

Hurricane Mk I, P3128, RF•A of 303 (Polish) Squadron, Northolt, August 1940
Dark Earth and Dark Green uppersurfaces, to the A Scheme pattern. Undersurfaces possibly in the correct shade of Sky. 49 inch Red/Blue upperwing roundels; 35 inch Red/White/Blue/Yellow fuselage roundels, and 50 inch underwing roundels, re-introduced in August 1940. The fin flash consisted of three 8 inch wide Red/White/Blue stripes extending 27 inches up the fin. The Medium Sea Grey Squadron codes were approximately 36 inches high. Note the angled Blue band across the rear fuselage which may have indicated a Flight Commander's aircraft, and the Polish 111 *Esk* Warsaw-Kosciuszko unit emblem on the mid fuselage.

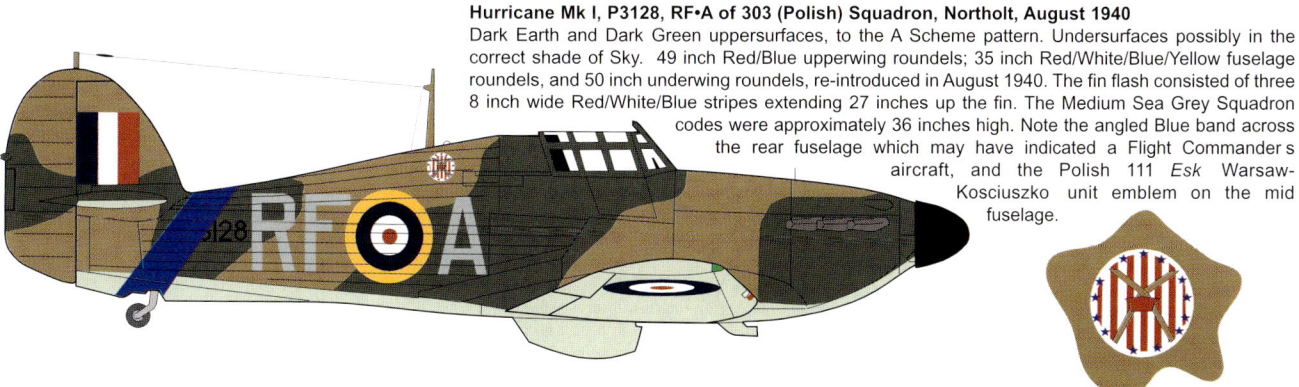

Hurricane Mk I, R4224, YB•C of 17 Squadron, North Weald, September 1940, flown by S/L A G Miller
Dark Earth and Dark Green uppersurfaces, to the B Scheme pattern. Undersurfaces appear to be in one of the Sky substitute colours - possibly the duck egg green shade - Eau de Nil BS 381 (1930) No 16, and In common with other machines from this unit, the spinner was painted in the underside colour which extended up nose and had a scalloped effect to the leading edges of the wings. 49 inch Red/Blue upperwing roundels; 35 inch Red/White/Blue/Yellow fuselage roundels, and 50 inch underwing roundels. The fin flash consisted of 9 inch wide Blue and White stripes with the entire front of the fin in Red. The Medium Sea Grey Squadron codes were approximately 30 inches high. Note the squadron leader's pennant under the cockpit.

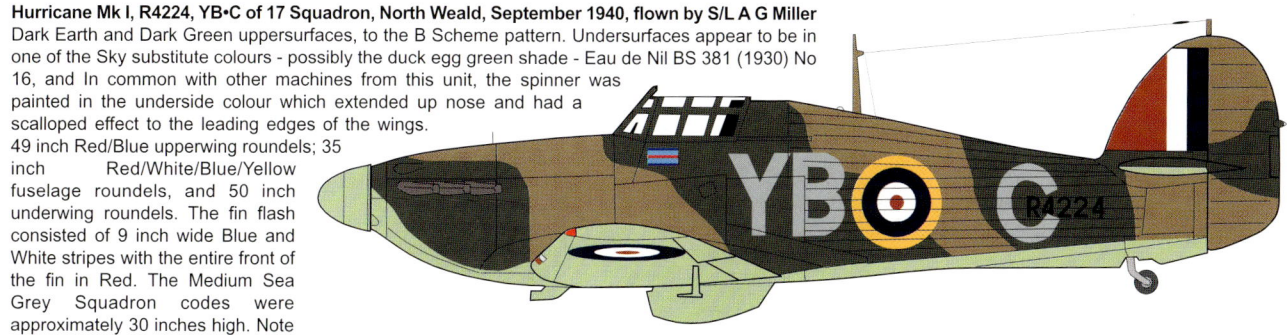

Hurricane Mk I, P3245, NN•Q of 310 (Czech) Squadron, Duxford, September 1940
Dark Earth and Dark Green uppersurfaces, to the B Scheme pattern. Undersurfaces possibly in the correct shade of Sky. 49 inch Red/Blue upperwing roundels; 35 inch Red/White/Blue/Yellow fuselage roundels (with a non-standard small Red centre), and 50 inch underwing roundels. The fin flash consisted of 9 inch wide Blue and White stripes with the entire front of the fin in Red. Unusually, the Squadron codes were white or a very light grey shade and approximately 30 inches high.

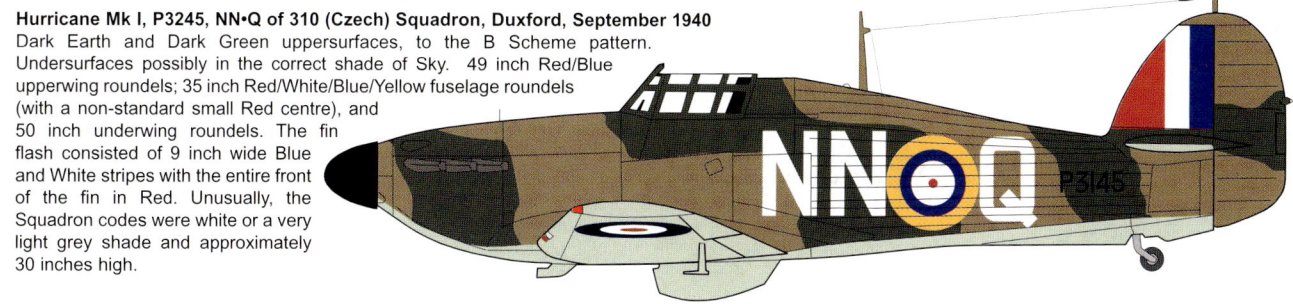

Hurricane Mk I, (serial unknown), KW•E of 615 Squadron, Northolt, October 1940
Dark Earth and Dark Green uppersurfaces, to the A Scheme pattern. Undersurfaces possibly in the correct shade of Sky. 49 inch Red/Blue upperwing roundels; 35 inch Red/White/Blue/Yellow fuselage roundels, and approximately 30 inch underwing roundels. The fin flash consisted of 9 inch wide Blue and White stripes with the entire front of the fin in Red. The Medium Sea Grey Squadron codes were approximately 30 inches high.

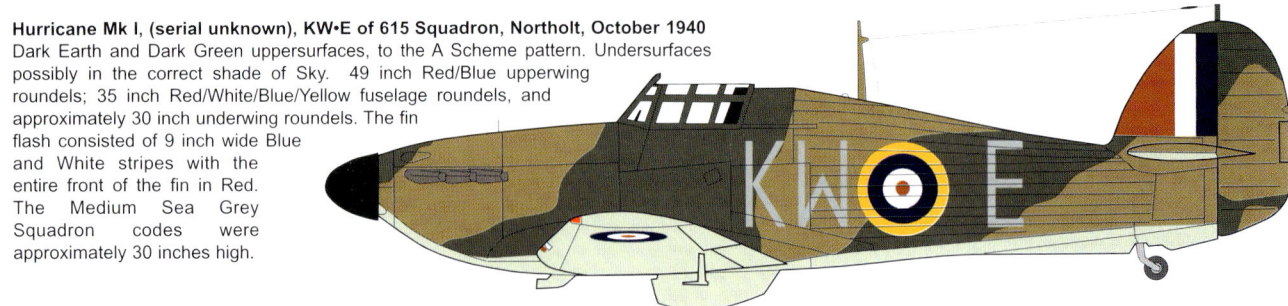

Hurricane Mk I, V6873, DT•O of 257 Squadron, North Weald, December 1940
Dark Earth and Dark Green uppersurfaces, to the B Scheme pattern. Undersurfaces were in one of the Sky substitute colours - possibly the duck egg blue shade - Sky Blue BS 381 (1930) No 1, with the port wing up to the fuselage centreline in Special Night - a recognition marking introduced in November 1940. 49 inch Red/Blue upperwing roundels; 35 inch Red/White/Blue/Yellow fuselage roundels, and 45 inch underwing roundels, the one under port wing thinly outlined in Yellow. The spinner and the rear fuselage tail band were in Air Ministry Sky Blue. Note the rearward position of the tail band partially extending on to the fin. The fin flash consisted of three 8 inch wide Red/White/Blue stripes extending 27 inches up the fin. The Medium Sea Grey Squadron codes were approximately 30 inches high.

Hurricane Mk I, (serial unknown), SD•O of 501 Squadron, Kenley, December 1940, flown by P/O K MacKenzie
Dark Earth and Dark Green uppersurfaces, to the A Scheme pattern. Sky ndersurfaces with the port wing up to the fuselage centreline in Special Night. 49 inch Red/Blue upperwing roundels; 35 inch Red/White/Blue/Yellow fuselage roundels, and 45 inch underwing roundels, the one under port wing thinly outlined in Yellow. The spinner and the rear fuselage tail band were in Air Ministry Sky Blue. The fin flash consisted of three 8 inch wide Red/White/Blue stripes extending 27 inches up the fin. The Medium Sea Grey Squadron codes were approximately 40 inches high.

Hurricane Mk I, V7104, UF•B of 601 Squadron, Northolt, early 1941
Dark Earth and Dark Green uppersurfaces, to the B Scheme pattern. Undersurfaces still in one of the Sky substitute colours - possibly the duck egg green shade - Eau de Nil BS 381 (1930) No 16, with the port wing up to the fuselage centreline in Special Night. 49 inch Red/Blue upperwing roundels; 35 inch Red/White/Blue/Yellow fuselage roundels, and 45 inch underwing roundels, the one under port wing thinly outlined in Yellow. The spinner and the rear fuselage tail band were in Air Ministry Sky Blue. Note how the tail band is truncated to avoid obliterating the serial number. The fin flash is the 24 inch x 27 inch style. The Medium Sea Grey Squadron codes are approximately 24 inches high.

Hurricane Mk I, V6701, JU•F of 111 Squadron, Dyce, February 1941
Dark Earth and Dark Green uppersurfaces, to the B Scheme pattern. Sky undersurfaces with the port wing up to the fuselage centreline in Special Night. 49 inch Red/Blue upperwing roundels; 35 inch Red/White/Blue/Yellow fuselage roundels, and approximately 30 inch underwing roundels, the one under port wing thinly outlined in Yellow. The spinner and the rear fuselage tail band were in Air Ministry Sky Blue. Note the rearward position of the tail band partially extending on to the fin. The fin flash consisted of 9 inch wide Blue and White stripes with the entire front of the fin in Red. The Medium Sea Grey Squadron codes are approximately 36 inches high.

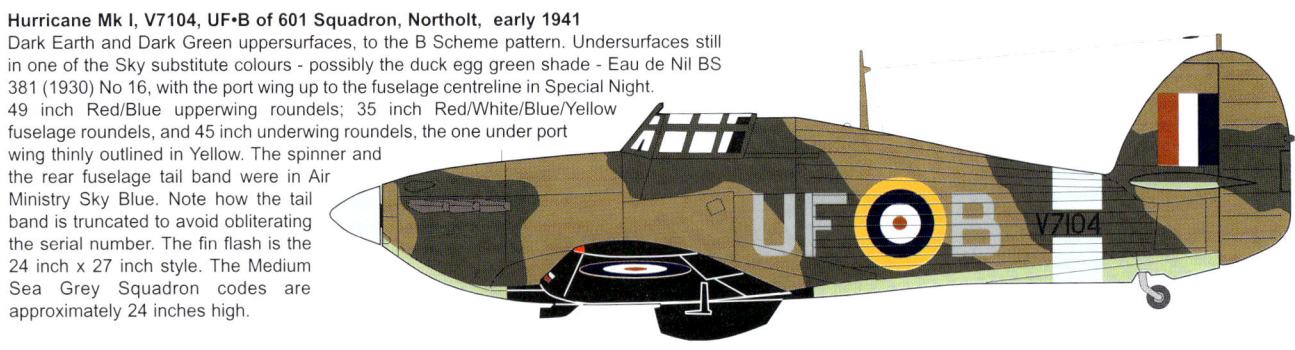

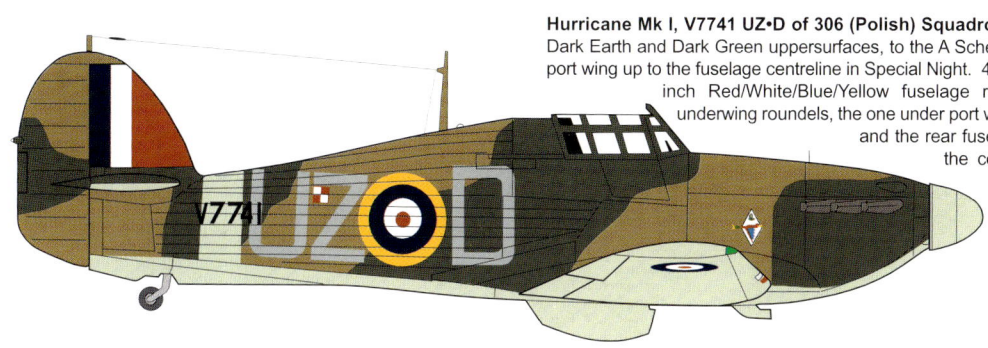

Hurricane Mk I, V7741 UZ•D of 306 (Polish) Squadron, Church Stanton, February 1941
Dark Earth and Dark Green uppersurfaces, to the A Scheme pattern. Sky undersurfaces with the port wing up to the fuselage centreline in Special Night. 49 inch Red/Blue upperwing roundels; 35 inch Red/White/Blue/Yellow fuselage roundels, and approximately 30 inch underwing roundels, the one under port wing thinly outlined in Yellow. The spinner and the rear fuselage tail band were probably applied in the correct shade of Sky. Note the slanting position of the tail band. The fin flash consisted of 9 inch wide Blue and White stripes with the entire front of the fin in Red. The Medium Sea Grey Squadron codes are approximately 36 inches high and were not perpendicular. Note the Polish national insignia marking on the rear fuselage and the *Torunski'* (City of Torun) Squadron badge on the cowling.

Hurricane Mk I, P2798, LK•A of 87 Squadron, Colerne, February 1941, flown by S/L Ian 'Widge' Gleed
Overall Special Night. 49 inch Red/Blue upperwing roundels; 49 inch Red/White/Blue/Yellow fuselage roundels, and approximately 30 inch underwing roundels. The fin flash consisted of 9 inch wide Blue and White stripes with the entire front of the fin in Red. The Medium Sea Grey Squadron codes are approximately 36 inches high, and the aircraft letter A had peeled badly. Note the Blue spinner, cowling front and rudder stripes, and the Squadron Leader's pennant under the windscreen.

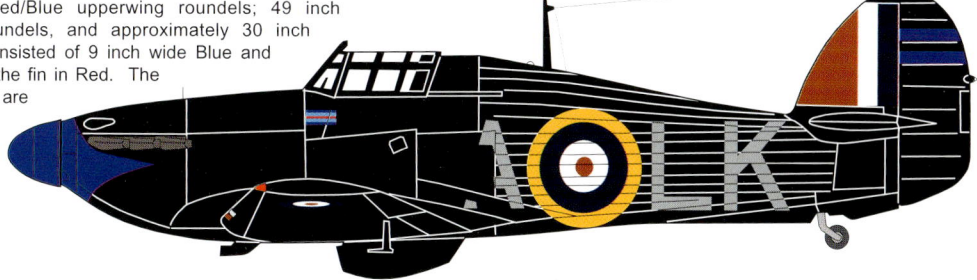

Hurricane Mk I, Vxxx8, XR•J of 71 Squadron, Kirton-in-Lindsey, early 1941
Dark Earth and Dark Green uppersurfaces, to the B Scheme pattern. Sky undersurfaces with the port wing up to the fuselage centreline in Special Night. 49 inch Red/Blue upperwing roundels; 35 inch Red/White/Blue/Yellow fuselage roundels, and approximately 45 inch underwing roundels, the one under port wing outlined in Yellow. The spinner and the rear fuselage tail band were probably applied in the correct shade of Sky. The fin flash is the 24 inch x 27 inch style. The Medium Sea Grey Squadron codes are approximately 30 inches high. This unit was the first Eagle Squadron, comprised of American volunteer pilots.

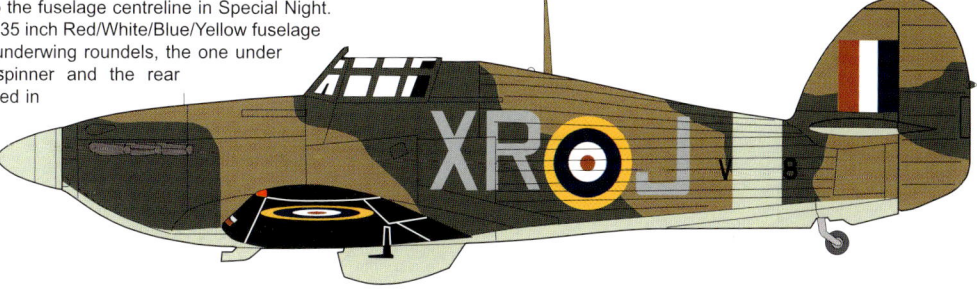

Hurricane Mk I, (serial unknown), FM•P of 257 Squadron, Coltishall, March 1941.
Dark Earth and Dark Green uppersurfaces, to the A Scheme pattern. Sky undersurfaces with the port wing up to the fuselage centreline in Special Night. 49 inch Red/Blue upperwing roundels; 35 inch Red/White/Blue/Yellow fuselage roundels, and approximately 30 inch underwing roundels, the one under port wing outlined in Yellow. The spinner and the rear fuselage tail band were probably applied in Air Ministry Sky Blue. Note the black rear portion to the spinner. The fin flash is the 24 inch x 27 inch style. The Medium Sea Grey Squadron codes are approximately 30 inches high, and were changed, (from the previous DT allocation), after photos were published in the press which identified the unit.

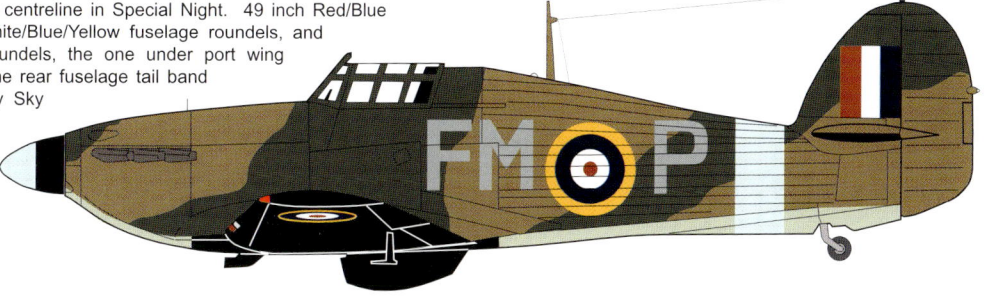

Hurricane Mk IIa, Z2703, KW•M of 615 Squadron, Kenley, May 1941
Dark Earth and Dark Green uppersurfaces, to the A Scheme pattern. A return to all Sky undersurfaces from 22 April 1941. 49 inch Red/Blue upperwing roundels; 35 inch Red/White/Blue/Yellow fuselage roundels, and approximately 30 inch underwing roundels, the one under port wing outlined in Yellow. The spinner and the rear fuselage tail band were probably applied in Air Ministry Sky Blue. Note the black rear plate to the spinner. The fin flash is the 24 inch x 27 inch style. The Medium Sea Grey Squadron codes are approximately 30 inches high. This was a presentation aircraft from the residents of the nearby town of Croydon, and carried the town's Coat of Arms on the mid fuselage.

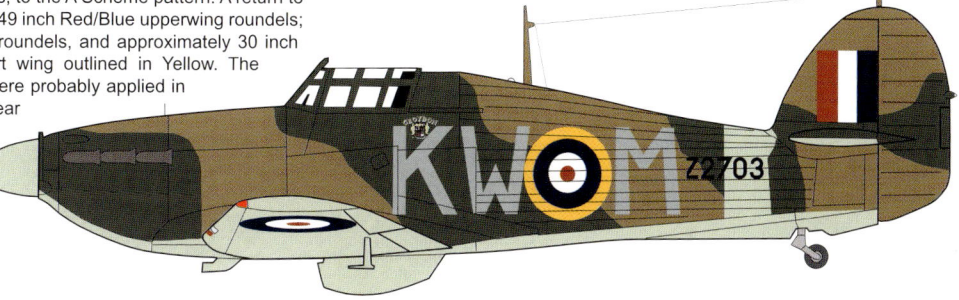

Hurricane Mk IIa, Z3239, AE•G of 402 Squadron (RCAF), Digby, May 1941, flown by S/L Bob Morrow
Dark Earth and Dark Green uppersurfaces, to the A Scheme pattern, with Sky undersurfaces. 49 inch Red/Blue upperwing roundels; 35 inch Red/White/Blue/Yellow fuselage roundels, and approximately 50 inch underwing roundels. The spinner and the rear fuselage tail band were Sky. The fin flash is the 24 inch x 27 inch style. The Medium Sea Grey Squadron codes are approximately 30 inches high.

Hurricane Mk I, P2827, PK•K of 315 (Polish) Squadron, Speke, June 1941
Dark Earth and Dark Green uppersurfaces, to the B Scheme pattern, with Sky undersurfaces. 49 inch Red/Blue upperwing roundels; 35 inch Red/White/Blue/Yellow fuselage roundels, and approximately 50 inch underwing roundels. The spinner and the (very uneven) rear fuselage tail band were Sky. The fin flash is the 24 inch x 27 inch style. The Medium Sea Grey Squadron codes are approximately 30 inches high. Note the Polish national insignia under the windscreen.

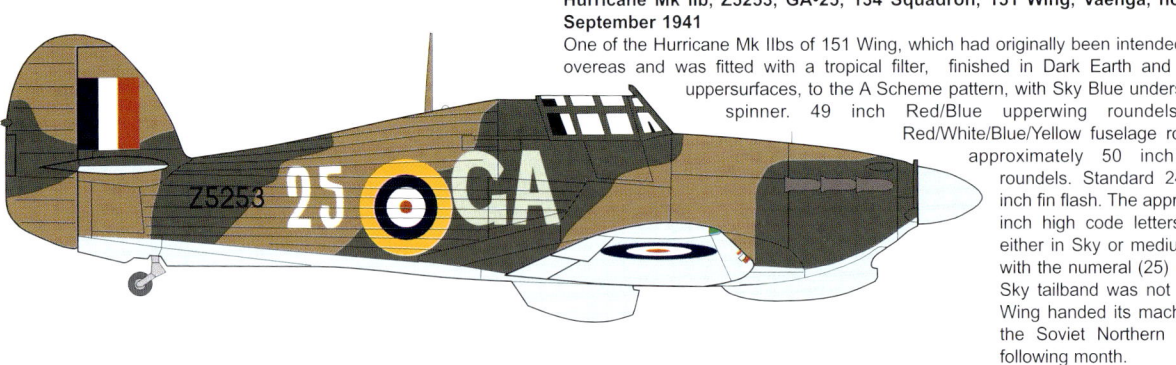

Hurricane Mk IIb, Z5253, GA•25, 134 Squadron, 151 Wing, Vaenga, north Russia, September 1941
One of the Hurricane Mk IIbs of 151 Wing, which had originally been intended for delivery overeas and was fitted with a tropical filter, finished in Dark Earth and Dark Green uppersurfaces, to the A Scheme pattern, with Sky Blue undersurfaces and spinner. 49 inch Red/Blue upperwing roundels; 35 inch Red/White/Blue/Yellow fuselage roundels, and approximately 50 inch underwing roundels. Standard 24 inch x 27 inch fin flash. The approximately 30 inch high code letters (GA) were either in Sky or medium Sea Grey with the numeral (25) in white. The Sky tailband was not applied. 151 Wing handed its machines over to the Soviet Northern Fleet in the following month.

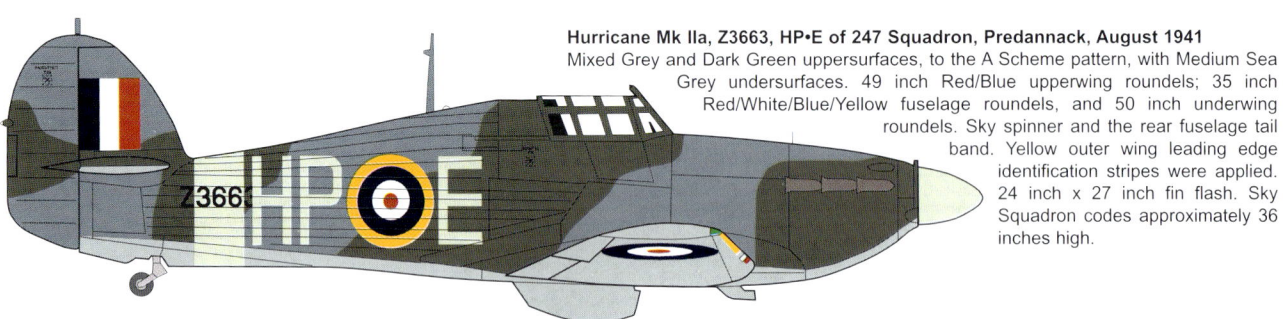

Hurricane Mk IIa, Z3663, HP•E of 247 Squadron, Predannack, August 1941
Mixed Grey and Dark Green uppersurfaces, to the A Scheme pattern, with Medium Sea Grey undersurfaces. 49 inch Red/Blue upperwing roundels; 35 inch Red/White/Blue/Yellow fuselage roundels, and 50 inch underwing roundels. Sky spinner and the rear fuselage tail band. Yellow outer wing leading edge identification stripes were applied. 24 inch x 27 inch fin flash. Sky Squadron codes approximately 36 inches high.

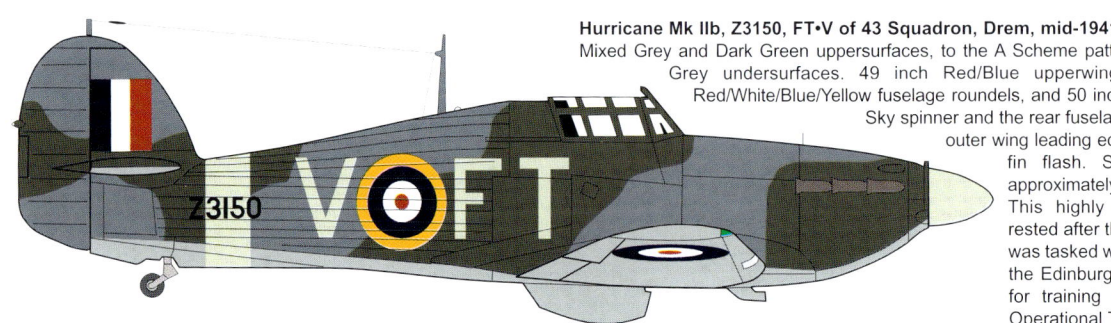

Hurricane Mk IIb, Z3150, FT•V of 43 Squadron, Drem, mid-1941
Mixed Grey and Dark Green uppersurfaces, to the A Scheme pattern, with Medium Sea Grey undersurfaces. 49 inch Red/Blue upperwing roundels; 35 inch Red/White/Blue/Yellow fuselage roundels, and 50 inch underwing roundels. Sky spinner and the rear fuselage tail band. No Yellow outer wing leading edges. 24 inch x 27 inch fin flash. Sky Squadron codes approximately 30 inches high.
This highly successful unit was rested after the Battle of Britain and was tasked with both the defence of the Edinburgh-Glasgow sector and for training pilots fresh from the Operational Training Units (OTUs).

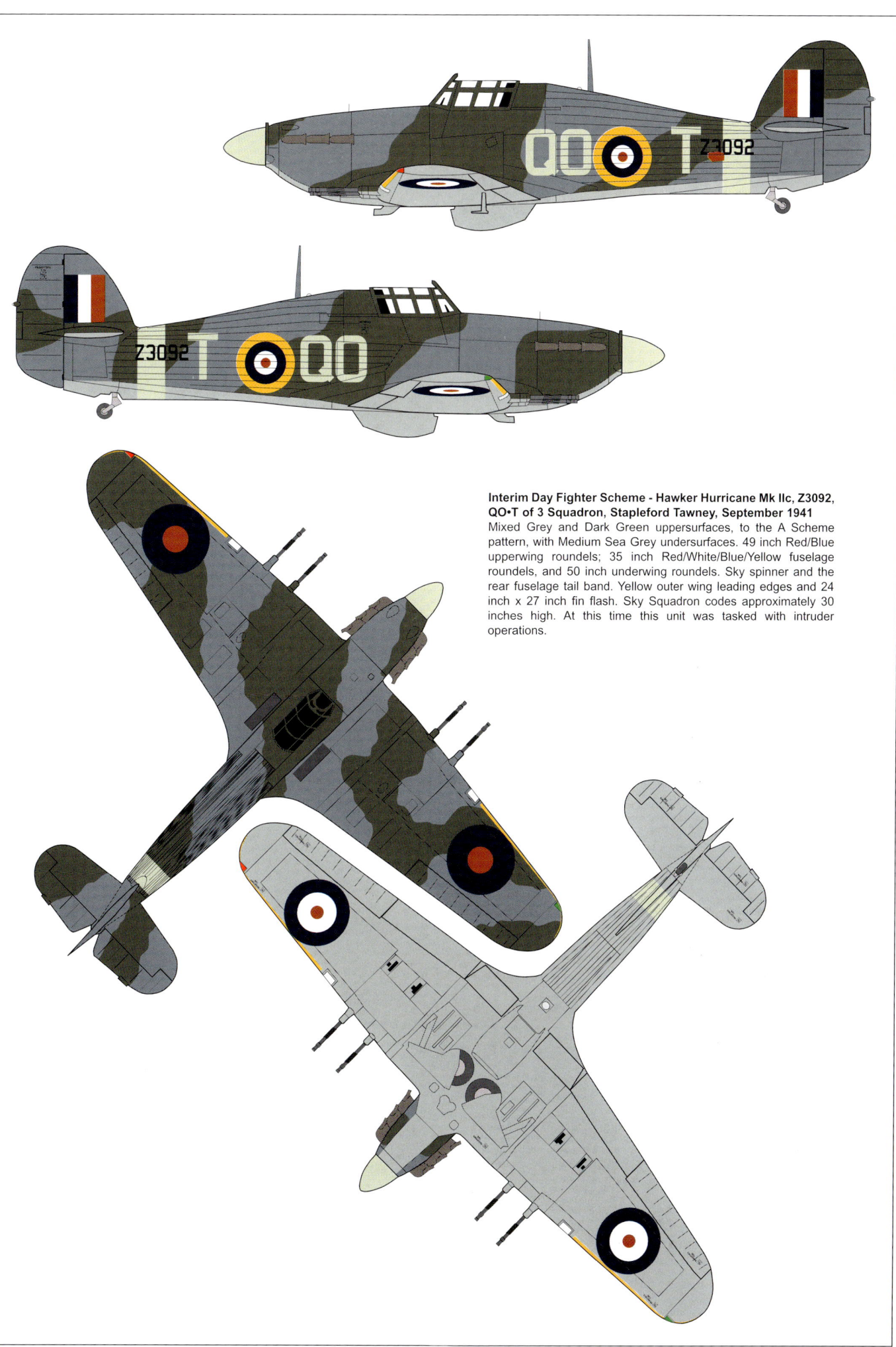

Interim Day Fighter Scheme - Hawker Hurricane Mk IIc, Z3092, QO•T of 3 Squadron, Stapleford Tawney, September 1941
Mixed Grey and Dark Green uppersurfaces, to the A Scheme pattern, with Medium Sea Grey undersurfaces. 49 inch Red/Blue upperwing roundels; 35 inch Red/White/Blue/Yellow fuselage roundels, and 50 inch underwing roundels. Sky spinner and the rear fuselage tail band. Yellow outer wing leading edges and 24 inch x 27 inch fin flash. Sky Squadron codes approximately 30 inches high. At this time this unit was tasked with intruder operations.

Hurricane Mk IIb, Z3356, UF•O of 601 Squadron, Northolt, autumn 1941
Mixed Grey and Dark Green uppersurfaces, to the A Scheme pattern, with Medium Sea Grey undersurfaces. 49 inch Red/Blue upperwing roundels; 35 inch Red/White/Blue/Yellow fuselage roundels, and 50 inch underwing roundels. Sky spinner and rear fuselage tail band - note position. Yellow outer wing leading edges and 24 inch x 27 inch fin flash - with 601 Sqn winged sword motif. Sky Squadron codes approximately 36 inches high. This unit's Hurribombers were used on Circus and Rhubarb operations until the type was replaced by the Airacobra in late 1941.

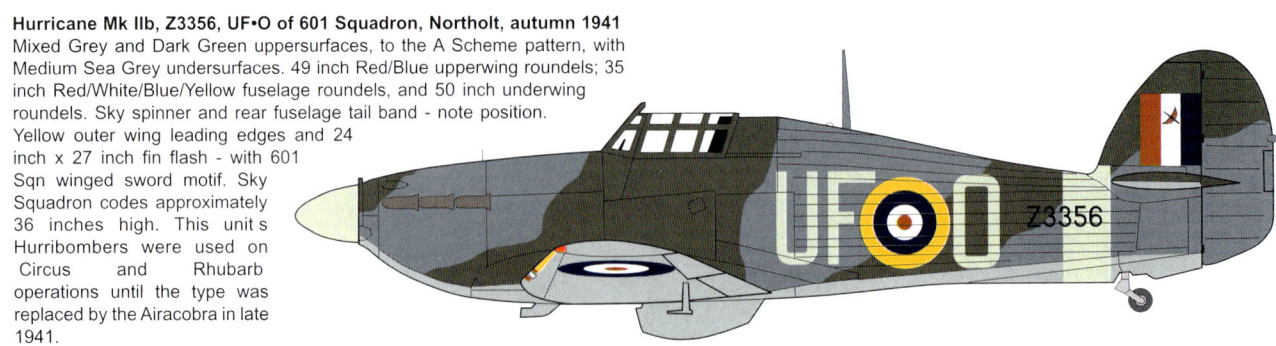

Hurricane Mk IIb, Z2633, NV•M of 79 Squadron, Fairwood Common, late 1941
Mixed Grey and Dark Green uppersurfaces, to the A Scheme pattern, with Medium Sea Grey undersurfaces. 49 inch Red/Blue upperwing roundels; 35 inch Red/White/Blue/Yellow fuselage roundels, and 50 inch underwing roundels. Sky spinner and rear fuselage tail band. Yellow outer wing leading edges and 24 inch x 27 inch fin flash. Sky Squadron codes approximately 36 inches high. This unit was tasked with the defence of the Midlands

Hurricane Mk IIb, Z3971, SW•S of 253 Squadron, Highbaldstow, late-1941
Overall Special Night. 49 inch Red/Blue upperwing roundels; 35 inch Red/White/Blue/Yellow fuselage roundels, and 50 inch underwing roundels. 24 inch x 27 inch fin flash. Medium Sea Grey 8 inch high serial number and 30 inch high Squadron codes. Note *Samastimas II* legend under port exhaust manifolds. This unit was tasked with the night defence of the Midlands.

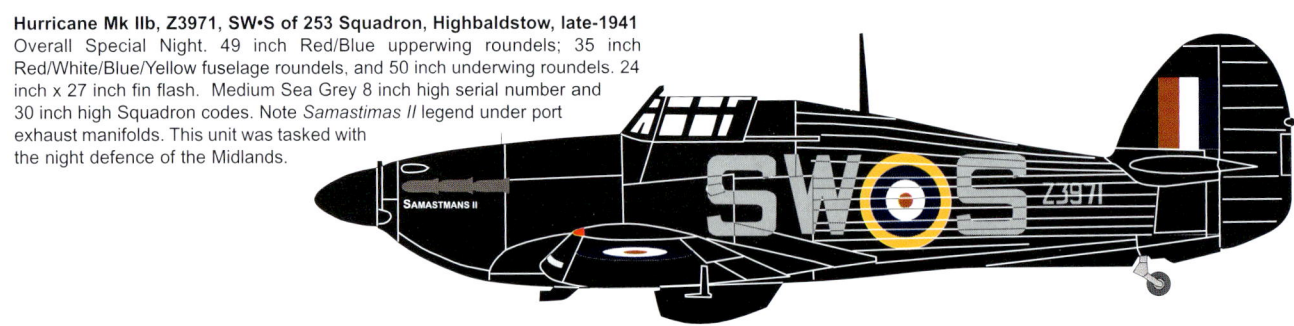

Hurricane Mk IIb, Z3658, YO•N of 401 Squadron (RCAF), Digby, July 1942
Ocean Grey and Dark Green uppersurfaces, to the A Scheme pattern, with Medium Sea Grey undersurfaces. 49 inch Red/Blue upperwing roundels; 35 inch Red/White/Blue/Yellow fuselage roundels, and 50 inch underwing roundels. Sky spinner and rear fuselage tail band. Yellow outer wing leading edges and 24 inch x 27 inch fin flash.

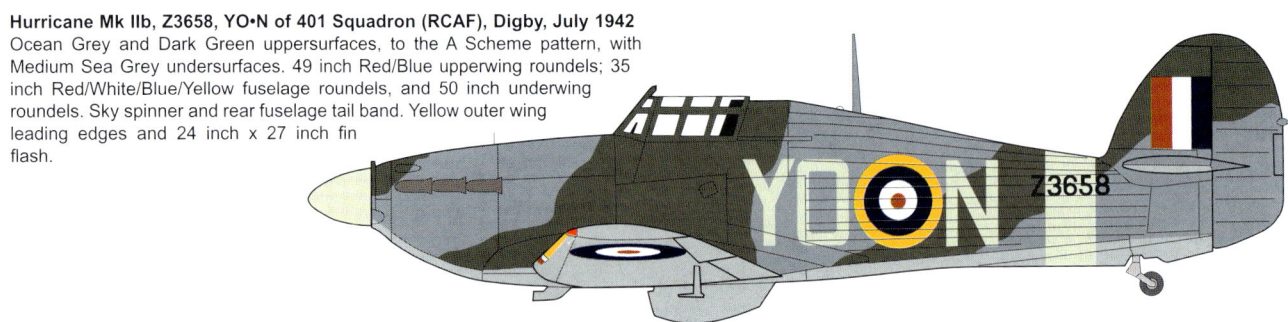

Hurricane Mk IIb, BE485, AE•W of 402 Squadron, Warmwell, 1942
Ocean Grey and Dark Green uppersurfaces, to the A Scheme pattern, with Medium Sea Grey undersurfaces. 49 inch Red/Blue upperwing roundels; 35 inch Red/White/Blue/Yellow fuselage roundels, and 50 inch underwing roundels. Sky spinner and rear fuselage tail band. Yellow outer wing leading edges and 24 inch x 27 inch fin flash. This unit's Hurribombers undertook Ramrod sorties over France, carrying two 250lb bombs. The aircraft letter was repeated in black on the cowling underside.

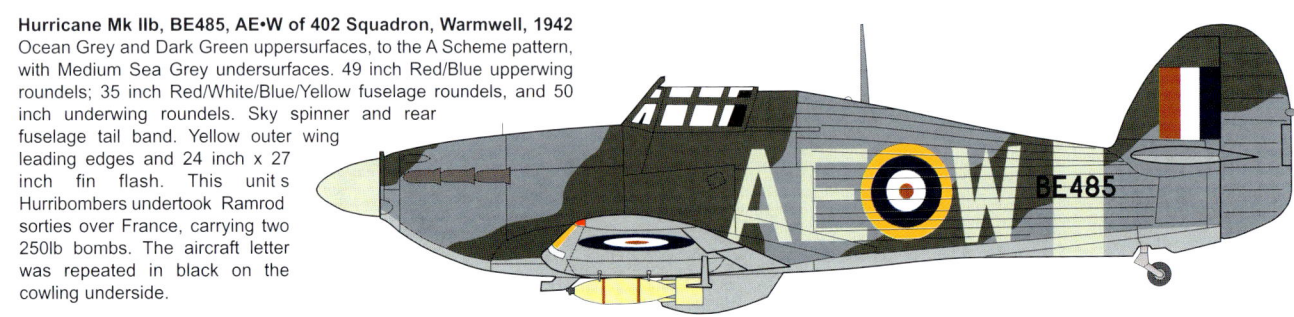

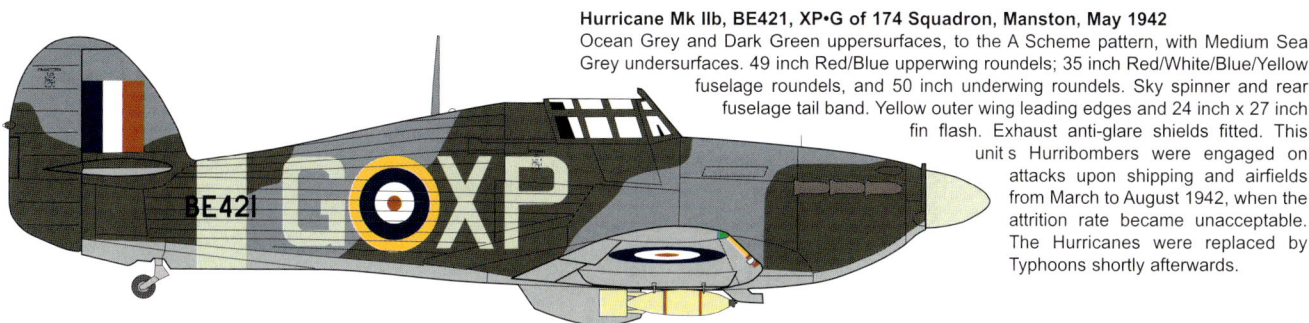

Hurricane Mk IIb, BE421, XP•G of 174 Squadron, Manston, May 1942
Ocean Grey and Dark Green uppersurfaces, to the A Scheme pattern, with Medium Sea Grey undersurfaces. 49 inch Red/Blue upperwing roundels; 35 inch Red/White/Blue/Yellow fuselage roundels, and 50 inch underwing roundels. Sky spinner and rear fuselage tail band. Yellow outer wing leading edges and 24 inch x 27 inch fin flash. Exhaust anti-glare shields fitted. This unit's Hurribombers were engaged on attacks upon shipping and airfields from March to August 1942, when the attrition rate became unacceptable. The Hurricanes were replaced by Typhoons shortly afterwards.

Hurricane Mk IIc, BD929, ZY•S of 247 Squadron, Exeter, 1942
Overall Special Night. This unit introduced the new style fuselage roundel, albeit in a reduced 18 inch overall diameter, which was given the official title National marking III, and the new style fin flash, titled Fin marking (i), again in a reduced size (18 inches square). Upperwing roundels probably remained at 49 inch Red/Blue - now termed National marking I. Underwing roundels were not applied.
The serial number and Squadron codes were applied in Red, and again in reduced size - (approx 4 inches and 18 inches respectively), with the codes positioned behind the roundel and separated by a hyphen. This unit undertook night Intruder and Roadstead operations.

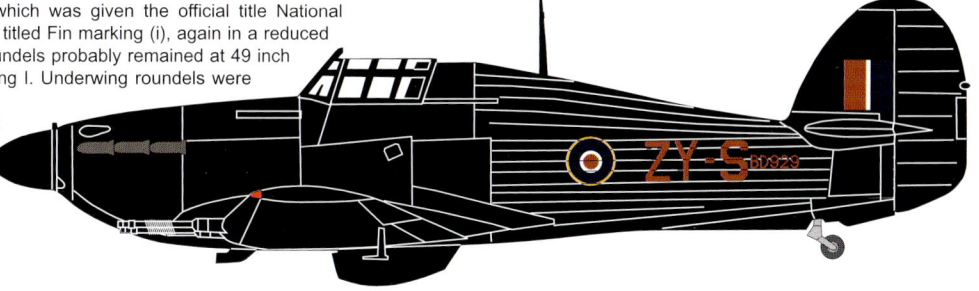

Hurricane Mk IIc, BE581, JX•E of 1 Squadron, Redhill, May 1942, flown by F/L K M Kuttlewascher
Illustrated in its original Overall Special Night scheme, with full size 36 inch diameter National marking III fuselage roundels and 24 inch x 24 inch Fin marking (i), with 49 inch Red/Blue National marking I upperwing roundels. The 36 inch high code letters and 8 inch high serial number was in Red.
(see 4-view on page 20)

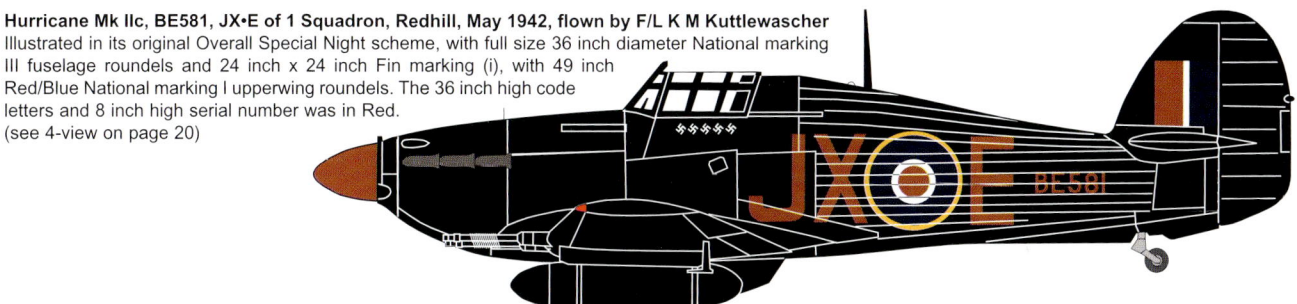

Hurricane Mk IIc, (serial unknown), LK•A of 87 Squadron, Warmwell, 1942
Uppersurface camouflage of Ocean Grey (or Mixed Grey) and Dark Green applied at unit level over the original, overall Special Night, scheme for the Dieppe raid in August 1942 and subsequent Mandolin intruder operations. National markings I, III and Fin marking (i) were applied. Medium Sea Grey or Sky, 30 inch high code letters.

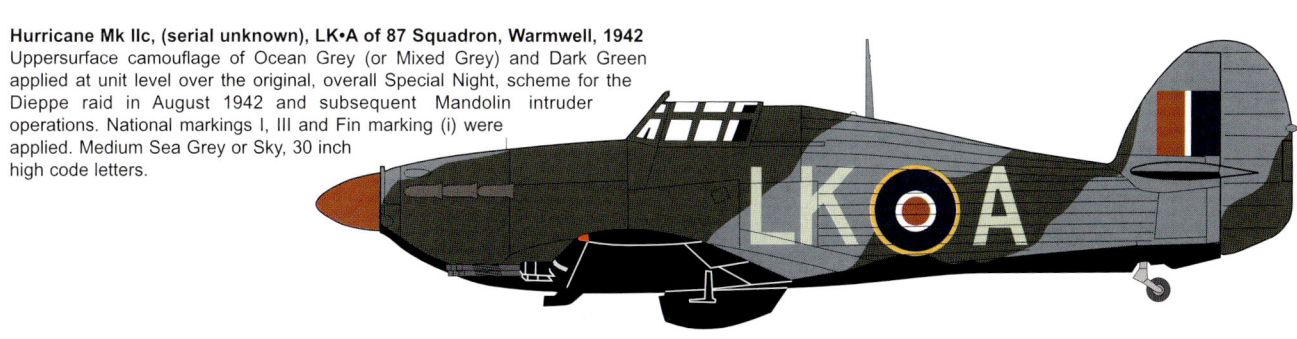

Hurricane Mk IIc, BN230, FT•A of 43 Squadron, Tangmere, August 1942, flown by S/L D A R G LeRoy du Vivier DFC
Ocean Grey and Dark Green uppersurfaces, to the A Scheme pattern, with Medium Sea Grey undersurfaces. 49 inch Red/Blue National marking I upperwing roundels; 36 inch Red/White/Blue/Yellow National marking III fuselage roundels, and 32 inch National marking II underwing roundels. Sky spinner and rear fuselage tail band. Yellow outer wing leading edges and 24 inch x 24 inch Fin marking (i). Used as air cover over Dieppe during Operation Jubilee.

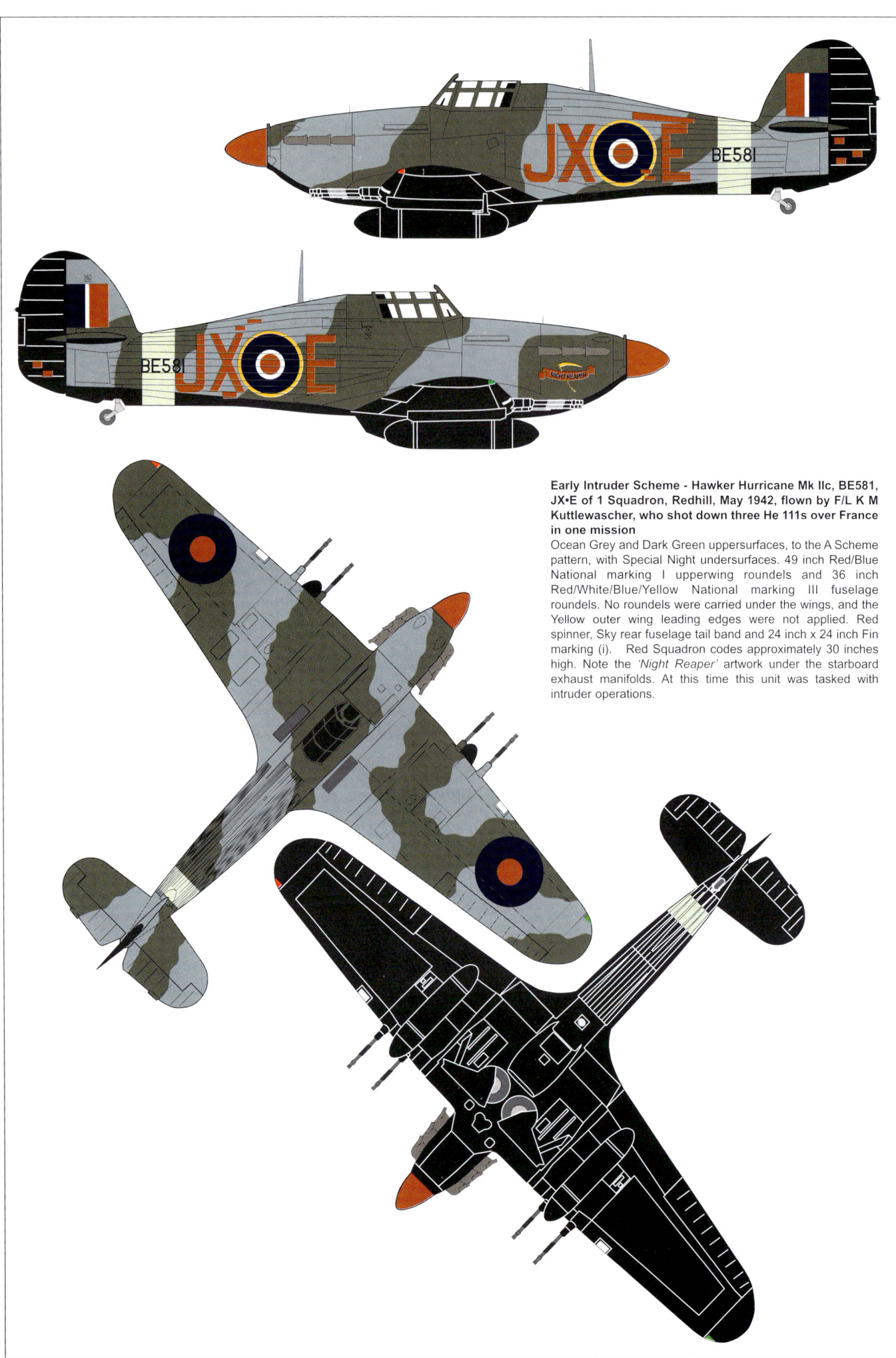

Early Intruder Scheme - Hawker Hurricane Mk IIc, BE581, JX•E of 1 Squadron, Redhill, May 1942, flown by F/L K M Kuttlewascher, who shot down three He 111s over France in one mission

Ocean Grey and Dark Green uppersurfaces, to the A Scheme pattern, with Special Night undersurfaces. 49 inch Red/Blue National marking I upperwing roundels and 36 inch Red/White/Blue/Yellow National marking III fuselage roundels. No roundels were carried under the wings, and the Yellow outer wing leading edges were not applied. Red spinner, Sky rear fuselage tail band and 24 inch x 24 inch Fin marking (i). Red Squadron codes approximately 30 inches high. Note the *'Night Reaper'* artwork under the starboard exhaust manifolds. At this time this unit was tasked with intruder operations.

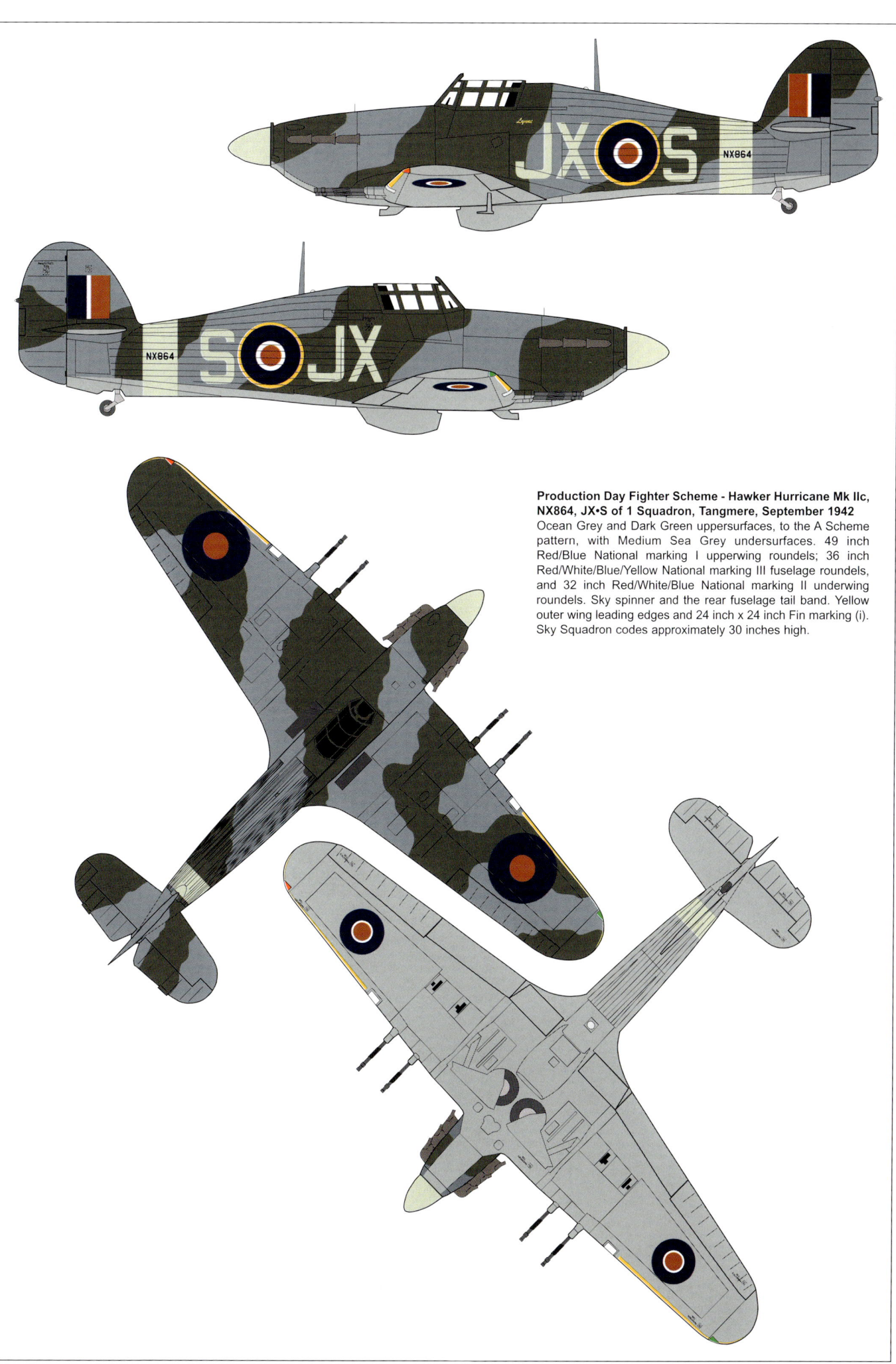

Production Day Fighter Scheme - Hawker Hurricane Mk IIc, NX864, JX•S of 1 Squadron, Tangmere, September 1942
Ocean Grey and Dark Green uppersurfaces, to the A Scheme pattern, with Medium Sea Grey undersurfaces. 49 inch Red/Blue National marking I upperwing roundels; 36 inch Red/White/Blue/Yellow National marking III fuselage roundels, and 32 inch Red/White/Blue National marking II underwing roundels. Sky spinner and the rear fuselage tail band. Yellow outer wing leading edges and 24 inch x 24 inch Fin marking (i). Sky Squadron codes approximately 30 inches high.

Hurricane Mk IId, KX561, FJ•G of 164 'Argentine-British' Squadron, Middle Wallop, June 1943
Ocean Grey and Dark Green uppersurfaces, to the C Scheme pattern, (with the uppersurface colours transposed) and Medium Sea Grey undersurfaces. 49 inch Red/Blue National marking I upperwing roundels; 36 inch Red/White/Blue/Yellow National marking III fuselage roundels, and 32 inch National marking II underwing roundels. Sky spinner and rear fuselage tail band, and 30 inch Sky codes. Yellow outer wing leading edges and 24 inch x 24 inch Fin marking (i). This version of the Hurricane carried two 40mm S guns in the anti-shipping role.

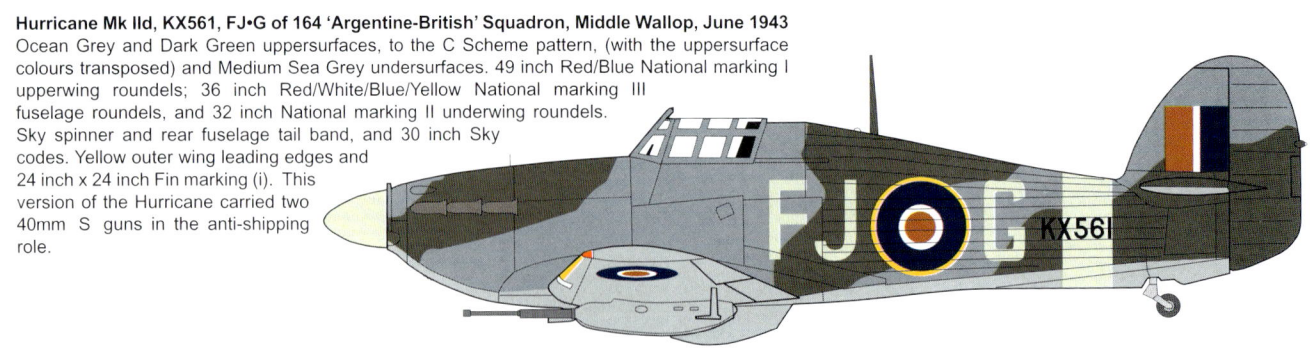

Hurricane Mk IIc, LF534, 6H•C of 1688 Bomber Defence Training Flight, Newmarket, April 1944
Ocean Grey and Dark Green uppersurfaces, to the A Scheme pattern, and Medium Sea Grey undersurfaces. 49 inch Red/Blue National marking I upperwing roundels; 36 inch Red/White/Blue/Yellow National marking III fuselage roundels, and 32 inch National marking II underwing roundels. Sky spinner and rear fuselage tail band. 24 inch and 36 inch Sky codes. Yellow outer wing leading edges and 24 inch x 24 inch Fin marking (i).

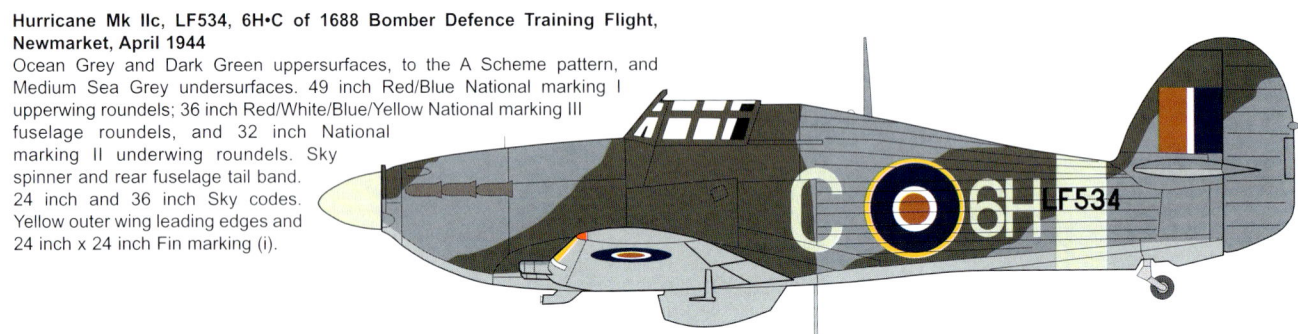

Hurricane Mk IIc, MW339, DR•H of 1555 Flight, the Northolt Air Despatch Letter Service, mid-1944
Ocean Grey and Dark Green uppersurfaces, to the A Scheme pattern, and Medium Sea Grey undersurfaces. 49 inch Red/Blue National marking I upperwing roundels; 36 inch Red/White/Blue/Yellow National marking III fuselage roundels, and 32 inch National marking II underwing roundels. Sky spinner and rear fuselage tail band. 24 inch Sky codes outlined in black. Yellow outer wing leading edges and 24 inch x 24 inch Fin marking (i).

Hurricane Mk IV, LD975, coded O of 351 (Yugoslav) Squadron, Prkos, Yugoslavia, April 1945
Ocean Grey and Dark Green uppersurfaces, to the A Scheme pattern, with either Sky Blue, Azure Blue or Light Mediterranean Blue undersurfaces. Red Yugoslavian stars were superimposed over modified standard RAF National markings. Red spinner, white code letter, Sky fuselage tail band and Yellow outer wing leading edges. The unit provided air support to the Yugoslav National Liberation Army.

Hurricane Mk IV, KZ188, coded C of 6 Squadron, Prkos, Yugoslavia, April 1945
Ocean Grey and Dark Green uppersurfaces, to the A Scheme pattern, with either Sky Blue, Azure Blue or Light Mediterranean Blue undersurfaces. 49 inch Red/White/Blue National marking IA upperwing roundels; 36 inch Red/White/Blue/Yellow National marking III fuselage roundels, and 32 inch National marking II underwing roundels. Sky spinner, rear fuselage tail band and individual aircraft letter. Yellow outer wing leading edges and 24 inch x 24 inch Fin marking (i). Fitted with rocket rails under the port wing and a long range tank under the starboard wing.

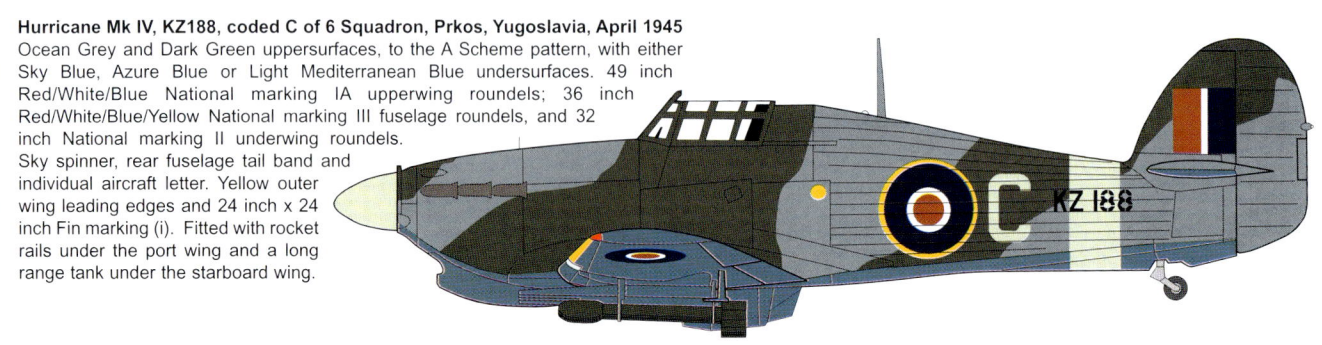

Hurricane Mk I, L2006, coded Y of 11 Group Pilot Pool, Sutton Bridge, 1939
Dark Earth and Dark Green uppersurfaces, in the B Scheme pattern, with Yellow undersurfaces and spinner. 49 inch Red/Blue upperwing roundels; approximately 40 inch Red/White/Blue/Yellow fuselage roundels made from R/W/B 25 inch roundel with a broader than usual Yellow outer ring. No underwing roundels or fin flashes. Red fuselage band. This unit became 6 Operational Training Unit in March 1940 and then 56 OTU in the following November. This machine remained at Sutton Bridge throughout and had the most accidents of any aircraft on the station!

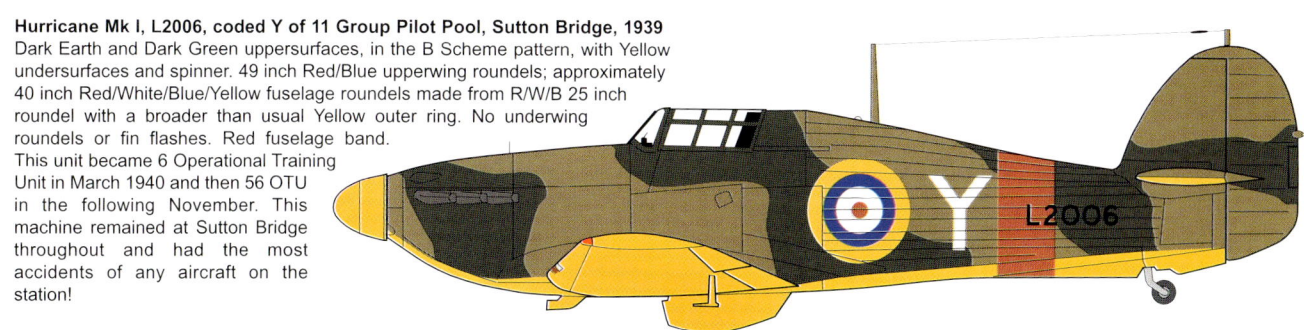

Hurricane Mk I, Z4791, 33•H of the Empire Central Flying School, Hullavington, September 1942
Extra Dark Sea Grey and Dark Slate Grey uppersurfaces, in the A Scheme pattern, with Sky undersurfaces. 49 inch Red/Blue National marking I upperwing roundels; 36 inch Red/White/Blue/Yellow National marking III fuselage roundels, and 32 inch National marking II underwing roundels. 24 inch x 24 inch Fin marking (i). Sky Blue spinner and rear fuselage tail band terminated at the bottom longeron line. 24 inch Sky Blue codes. Note unidentified artwork/badge on port cowling side.

Hurricane Mk I, P3039, PA•J of 55 Operational Training Unit, (OTU), Aston Down, 1942
Ocean Grey and Dark Green uppersurfaces, to the A Scheme pattern, and Medium Sea Grey undersurfaces. 49 inch Red/Blue National marking I upperwing roundels; 36 inch Red/White/Blue/Yellow National marking III fuselage roundels, and 32 inch National marking II underwing roundels. Sky spinner and rear fuselage tail band. 36 inch Sky codes. Yellow outer wing leading edges and 24 inch x 24 inch Fin marking (i).

Hurricane Mk X, AG162, EH•W of 55 Operational Training Unit (OTU), Usworth, 1942-43
Ocean Grey and Dark Green uppersurfaces, to the A Scheme pattern, and Medium Sea Grey undersurfaces. 49 inch Red/Blue National marking I upperwing roundels; 36 inch Red/White/Blue/Yellow National marking III fuselage roundels, and 32 inch National marking II underwing roundels. Sky spinner and rear fuselage tail band. 30 inch Sky codes. Yellow outer wing leading edges and 24 inch x 24 inch Fin marking (i).

Hurricane Mk I, V7173, MF•X34 of 59 Operational Training Unit (OTU), Turnhouse, 1943
Ocean Grey and Dark Green uppersurfaces, to the C Scheme pattern, (uppersurface colours transposed), and Medium Sea Grey undersurfaces. Note the natural metal canopy framing. 49 inch Red/Blue National marking I upperwing roundels; 36 inch Red/White/Blue/Yellow National marking III fuselage roundels, and 32 inch National marking II underwing roundels. Sky spinner and rear fuselage tail band. Approximately 20 inch white codes. Yellow outer wing leading edges and 24 inch x 24 inch Fin marking (i).

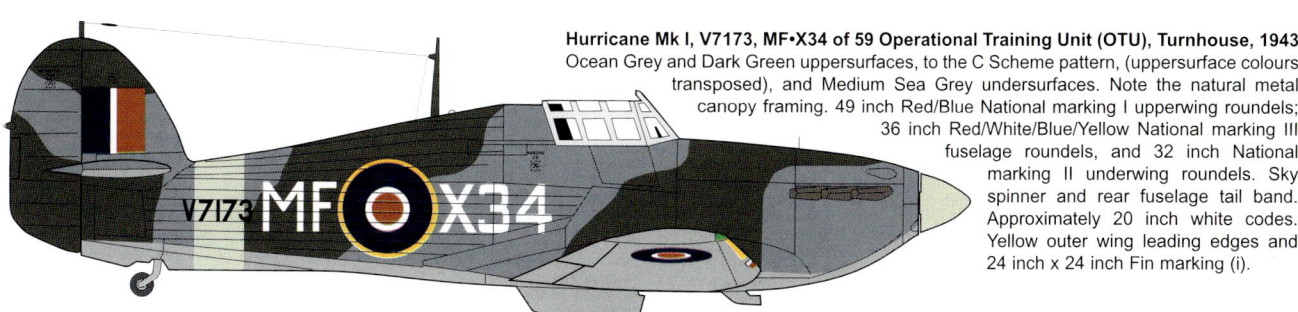

Hurricane Mk I, P2992, coded P of 527 Squadron, Castle Camps, 1943
Overall orange-red. 49 inch Red/Blue National marking I upperwing roundels; 36 inch Red/White/Blue/Yellow National marking III fuselage roundels, and 32 inch National marking II underwing roundels. 24 inch x 24 inch Fin marking (i) with the front (Red) portion thinly outlined in white. Black serial number and individual aircarft letter. This unit was involved in the calibration of radar, homing and blind-landing instrumentation.

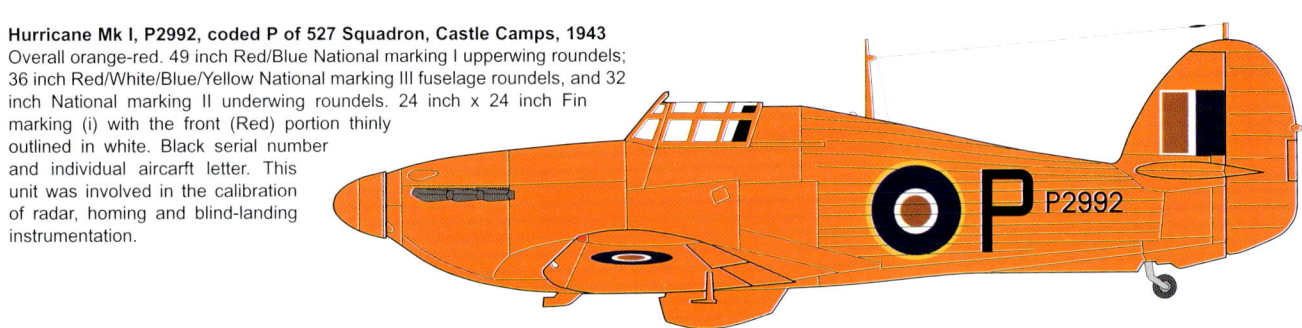

Hurricane Mk X, AG111, HK•G of the Fighter Leaders School, Millfield, January 1944
Ocean Grey and Dark Green uppersurfaces, to the A Scheme pattern, with Medium Sea Grey undersurfaces. 49 inch Red/Blue National marking I upperwing roundels; 36 inch Red/White/Blue/Yellow National marking III fuselage roundels, and 32 inch National marking II underwing roundels. Sky spinner and rear fuselage tail band. 30 inch Sky codes. Yellow outer wing leading edges and 24 inch x 24 inch Fin marking (i).

Hurricane Mk IIc, LF380, FI•D of 83 Operational Training Unit (OTU), Peplow, mid-1944
Ocean Grey and Dark Green uppersurfaces, to the A Scheme pattern, with Medium Sea Grey undersurfaces. 49 inch Red/Blue National marking I upperwing roundels; 36 inch Red/White/Blue/Yellow National marking III fuselage roundels, and 32 inch National marking II underwing roundels. Sky spinner and rear fuselage tail band. 18 inch White codes. Yellow outer wing leading edges and 24 inch x 24 inch Fin marking (i). 18 inch wide Black and White AEAF Invasion Stripes around rear fuselage, partially obliterating the Sky tail band.

Hurricane Mk (Met) IIc, (serial unknown), 50•X of 521 Squadron, Docking, September 1944
Ocean Grey and Dark Green uppersurfaces, to the A Scheme pattern, with Medium Sea Grey undersurfaces. 49 inch Red/Blue National marking I upperwing roundels; 36 inch Red/White/Blue/Yellow National marking III fuselage roundels, and 32 inch National marking II underwing roundels. Sky spinner and rear fuselage tail band. Approximately 40 inch Sky codes. Yellow outer wing leading edges and 24 inch x 24 inch Fin marking (i). This unit performed vital meteorological sorties, in support of all operational and air-sea rescue units.

Hurricane Mk XII, JS290, WN•P of 527 Squadron, Digby, 1945
Ocean Grey and Dark Green uppersurfaces, to the A Scheme pattern, with Medium Sea Grey undersurfaces. 49 inch Red/Blue National marking I upperwing roundels; 36 inch Red/White/Blue/Yellow National marking III fuselage roundels, and 32 inch National marking II underwing roundels. Red spinner and Sky rear fuselage tail band. Approximately 40 inch Sky codes. Yellow outer wing leading edges and 24 inch x 24 inch Fin marking (i).

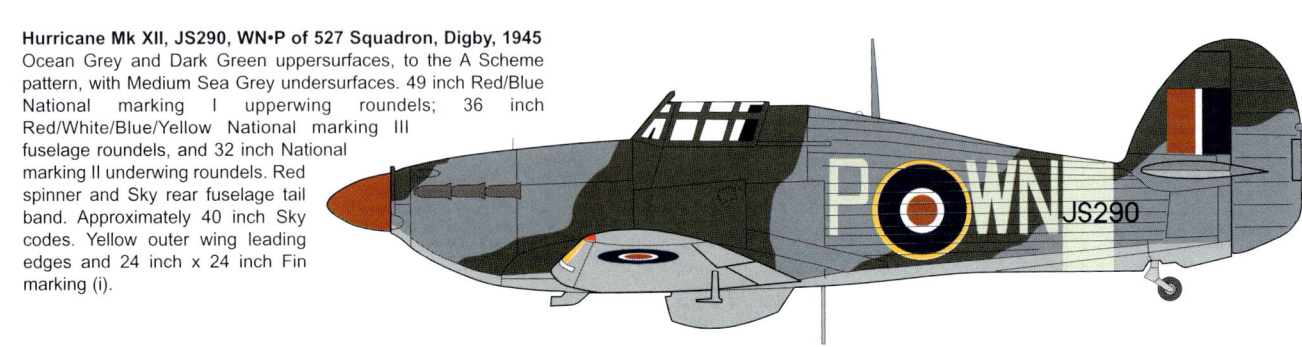

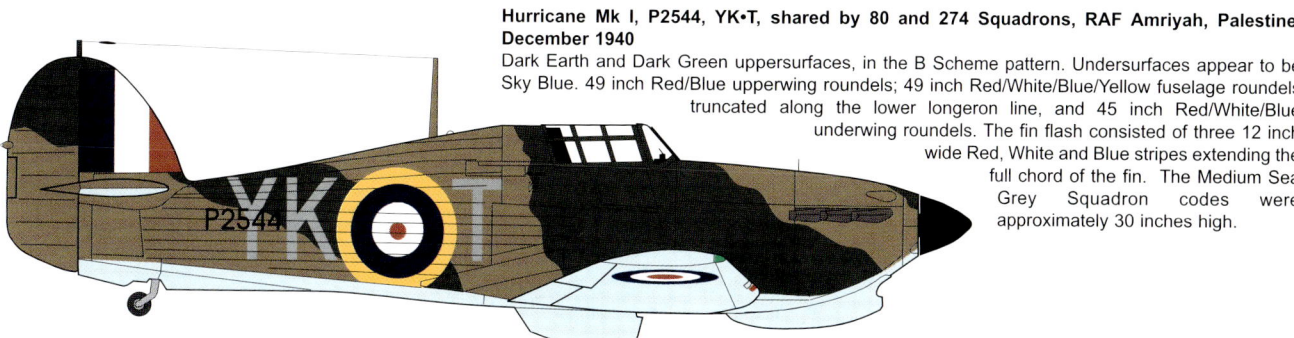

Hurricane Mk I, P2544, YK•T, shared by 80 and 274 Squadrons, RAF Amriyah, Palestine, December 1940
Dark Earth and Dark Green uppersurfaces, in the B Scheme pattern. Undersurfaces appear to be Sky Blue. 49 inch Red/Blue upperwing roundels; 49 inch Red/White/Blue/Yellow fuselage roundels truncated along the lower longeron line, and 45 inch Red/White/Blue underwing roundels. The fin flash consisted of three 12 inch wide Red, White and Blue stripes extending the full chord of the fin. The Medium Sea Grey Squadron codes were approximately 30 inches high.

Hurricane Mk I, 289 coded 'A' of 3 Squadron, South African Air Force, Abyssinia, mid-1940
Dark Earth and Dark Green uppersurfaces, in the A Scheme pattern. Undersurfaces appear to be Sky Blue. 49 inch Orange/Blue upperwing roundels; 35 inch Orange/White/Blue/Yellow fuselage roundels, and 45 inch Orange/White/Blue underwing roundels. The fin flash consisted of two 9 inch wide White and Blue stripes with the entire front of the fin in SAAF Orange. The Medium Sea Grey code letter was approximately 30 inches high. Note the artwork on the nose. No 3 Sqn SAAF was active against Italian forces during the East African campaign in Abyssinia, Somaliland and Eritrea.

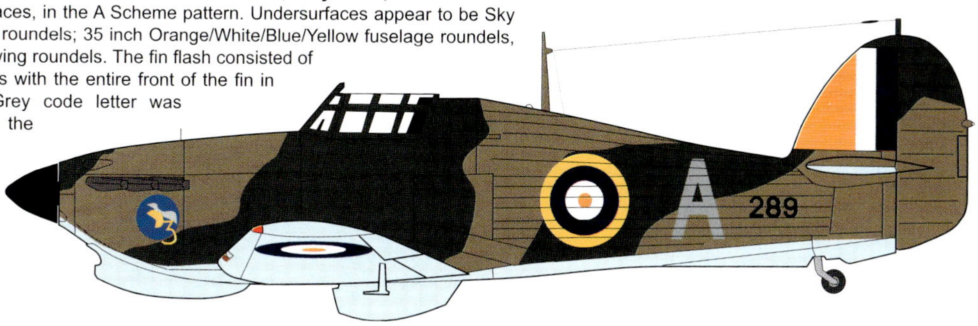

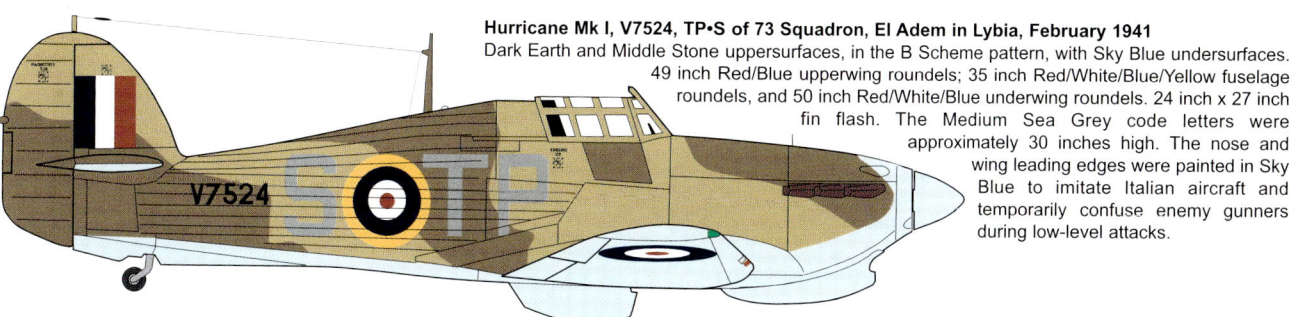

Hurricane Mk I, V7524, TP•S of 73 Squadron, El Adem in Lybia, February 1941
Dark Earth and Middle Stone uppersurfaces, in the B Scheme pattern, with Sky Blue undersurfaces. 49 inch Red/Blue upperwing roundels; 35 inch Red/White/Blue/Yellow fuselage roundels, and 50 inch Red/White/Blue underwing roundels. 24 inch x 27 inch fin flash. The Medium Sea Grey code letters were approximately 30 inches high. The nose and wing leading edges were painted in Sky Blue to imitate Italian aircraft and temporarily confuse enemy gunners during low-level attacks.

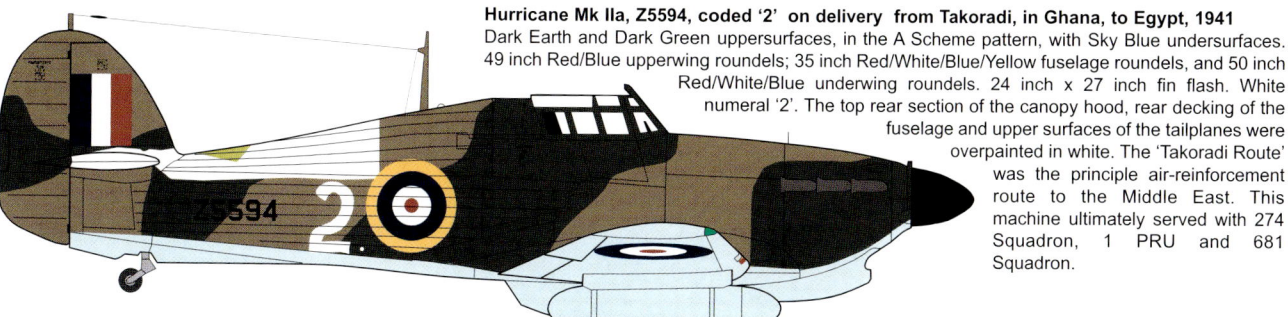

Hurricane Mk IIa, Z5594, coded '2' on delivery from Takoradi, in Ghana, to Egypt, 1941
Dark Earth and Dark Green uppersurfaces, in the A Scheme pattern, with Sky Blue undersurfaces. 49 inch Red/Blue upperwing roundels; 35 inch Red/White/Blue/Yellow fuselage roundels, and 50 inch Red/White/Blue underwing roundels. 24 inch x 27 inch fin flash. White numeral '2'. The top rear section of the canopy hood, rear decking of the fuselage and upper surfaces of the tailplanes were overpainted in white. The 'Takoradi Route' was the principle air-reinforcement route to the Middle East. This machine ultimately served with 274 Squadron, 1 PRU and 681 Squadron.

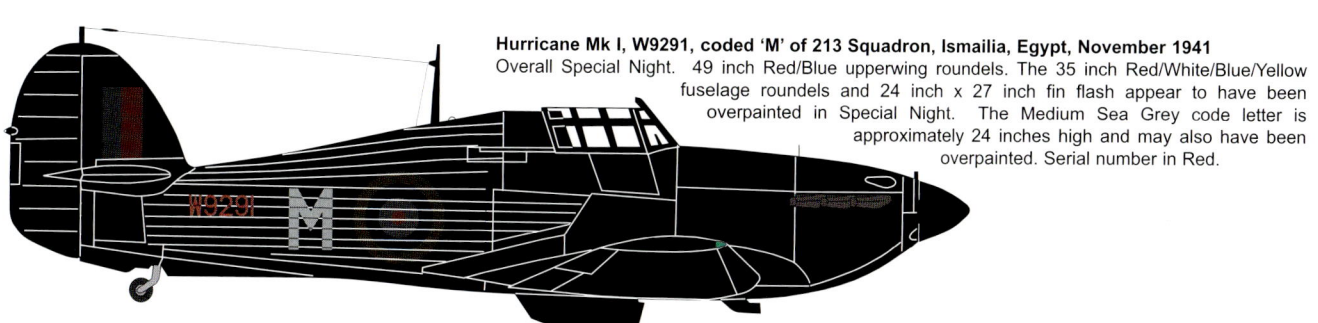

Hurricane Mk I, W9291, coded 'M' of 213 Squadron, Ismailia, Egypt, November 1941
Overall Special Night. 49 inch Red/Blue upperwing roundels. The 35 inch Red/White/Blue/Yellow fuselage roundels and 24 inch x 27 inch fin flash appear to have been overpainted in Special Night. The Medium Sea Grey code letter is approximately 24 inches high and may also have been overpainted. Serial number in Red.

Hurricane Mk I, P3731, 'J' of 261 Squadron, Ta Kali, Malta, mid-1941
Dark Earth and Middle Stone uppersurfaces, in the A Scheme pattern, with Sky Blue undersurfaces. 49 inch Red/Blue upperwing roundels; 35 inch Red/White/Blue/Yellow fuselage roundels, and 40 inch Red/White/Blue underwing roundels. The fin flash consisted of three 12 inch wide Red, White and Blue stripes extending the full chord of the fin. The code letter is approximately 24 inches high in white. This machine was one of several flown-off from the carrier, *HMS Argus* as part of urgently needed reinforcements to Malta.

Hurricane Mk II, Z2961, 'K' of 185 Squadron, Hal Far, Malta, May 1941
Dark Green and Middle Stone uppersurfaces, in the A Scheme pattern, with Sky Blue undersurfaces. 49 inch Red/Blue upperwing roundels; 35 inch Red/White/Blue/Yellow fuselage roundels, and 50 inch Red/White/Blue underwing roundels. 24 inch x 27 inch fin flash. The code letter is approximately 24 inches high in Medium Sea Grey.

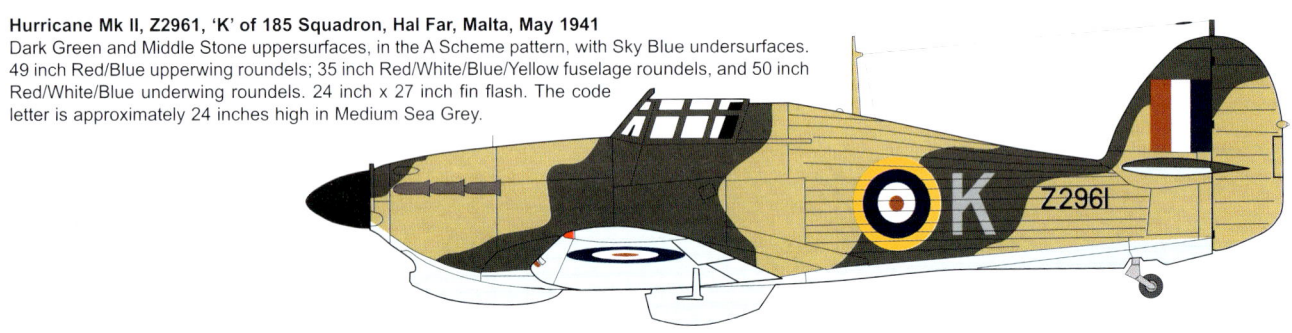

Hurricane Mk II, Z2402, GL•P of 185 Squadron, Hal Far, Malta, May 1941
Dark Green and Middle Stone uppersurfaces, in the B Scheme pattern, with Sky Blue undersurfaces. 49 inch Red/Blue upperwing roundels; 35 inch Red/White/Blue/Yellow fuselage roundels, and 50 inch Red/White/Blue underwing roundels. 24 inch x 27 inch fin flash. The code letters are approximately 18 inches high in white.

Hurricane Mk IIa, Z2827, 'M' of the Night Fighting Unit, Ta' Qali, Malta, July 1941
Dark Earth and Middle Stone uppersurfaces, in an in-service repaint non-standard pattern, with Special Night undersurfaces. 49 inch Red/Blue upperwing roundels; 35 inch Red/White/Blue/Yellow fuselage roundels, and 40 inch Red/White/Blue underwing roundels. 24 inch x 27 inch fin flash. Spinner could be Sky and the code letter is approximately 30 inches high in Medium Sea Grey.

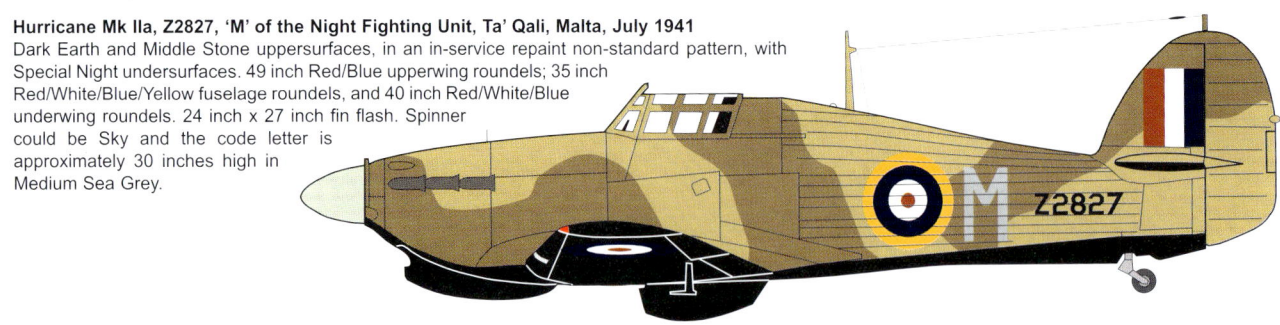

Hurricane Mk IIb, BG737 of the Malta Night Fighter Unit, Ta' Qali, Malta, July 1941
Overall Special Night. 49 inch Red/Blue upperwing roundels, 35 inch Red/Blue fuselage roundels and 50 inch Red/Blue underwing roundels. Standard Red/White/Blue 24 inch x 27 inch fin flash. Serial number in white.

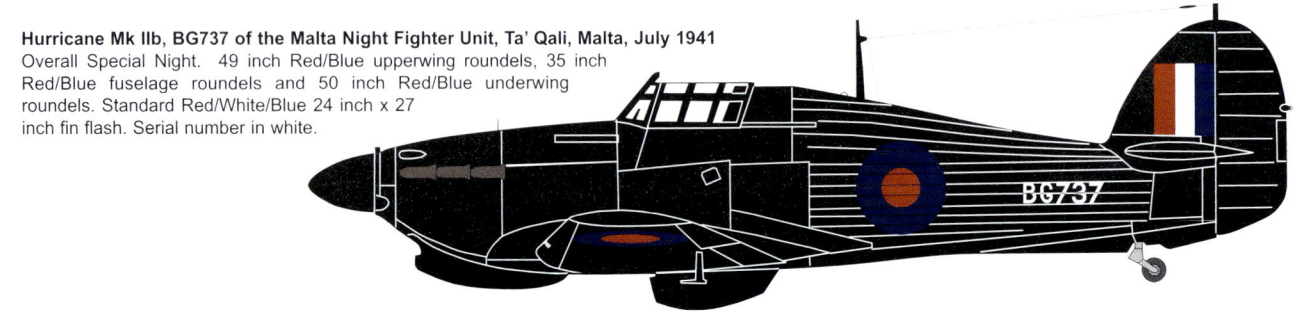

National markings styles, variations and sizes

 Air Marshal
 Air Vice-Marshal
 Air Commodore
 Group Captain
 Wing Commander
 Squadron Leader

 25 inch
 35 inch
 35 inch
 45 inch
 35 inch
 49 inch
 15 inch
 25 inch
 35 inch
 49 inch

 National marking II — 32 inch
 National marking III — 36 inch
 SEAC — 18 inch SEAC

Early serial number styles

 Gloster style.
 Hawker style
 No.1 Civilian Repair Unit style.

Fin marking and fuselage tail band styles

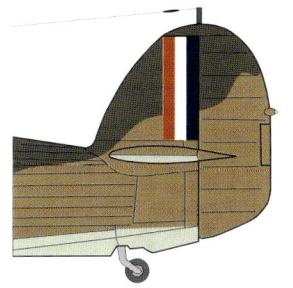 5 inch stripes
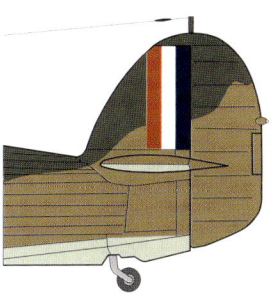 6 inch stripes
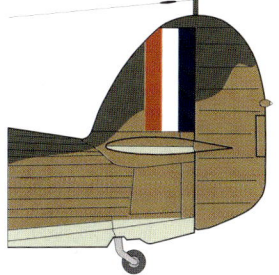 7 inch stripes

Fin marking styles 1940 to early 1941

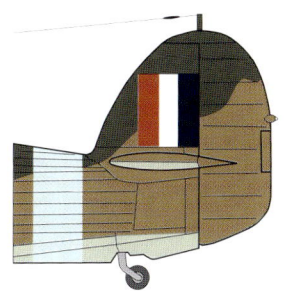
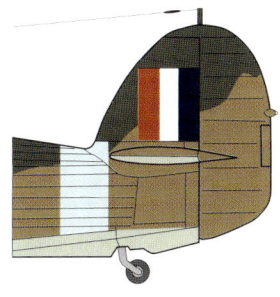
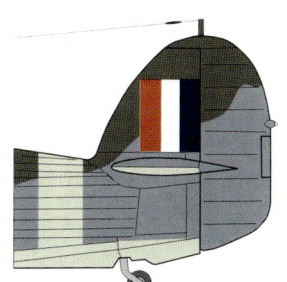
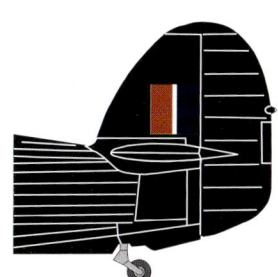

Fin markings and tail band styles late 1940 to early 1942

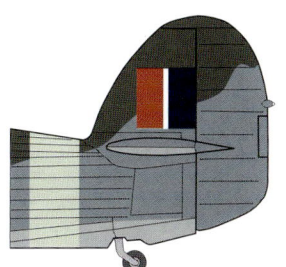 Fin marking (i)
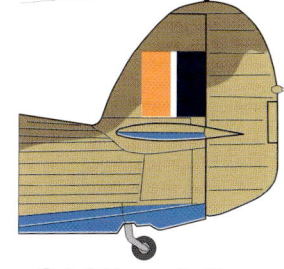 SAAF variation
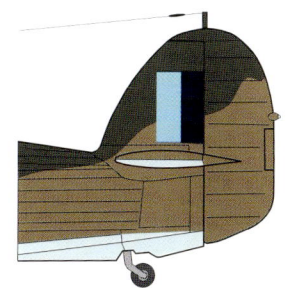 SEAC fin flash/Special i/d marking
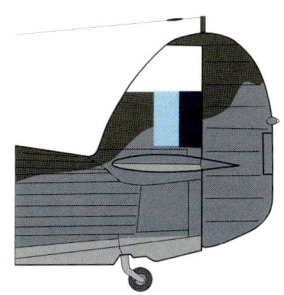

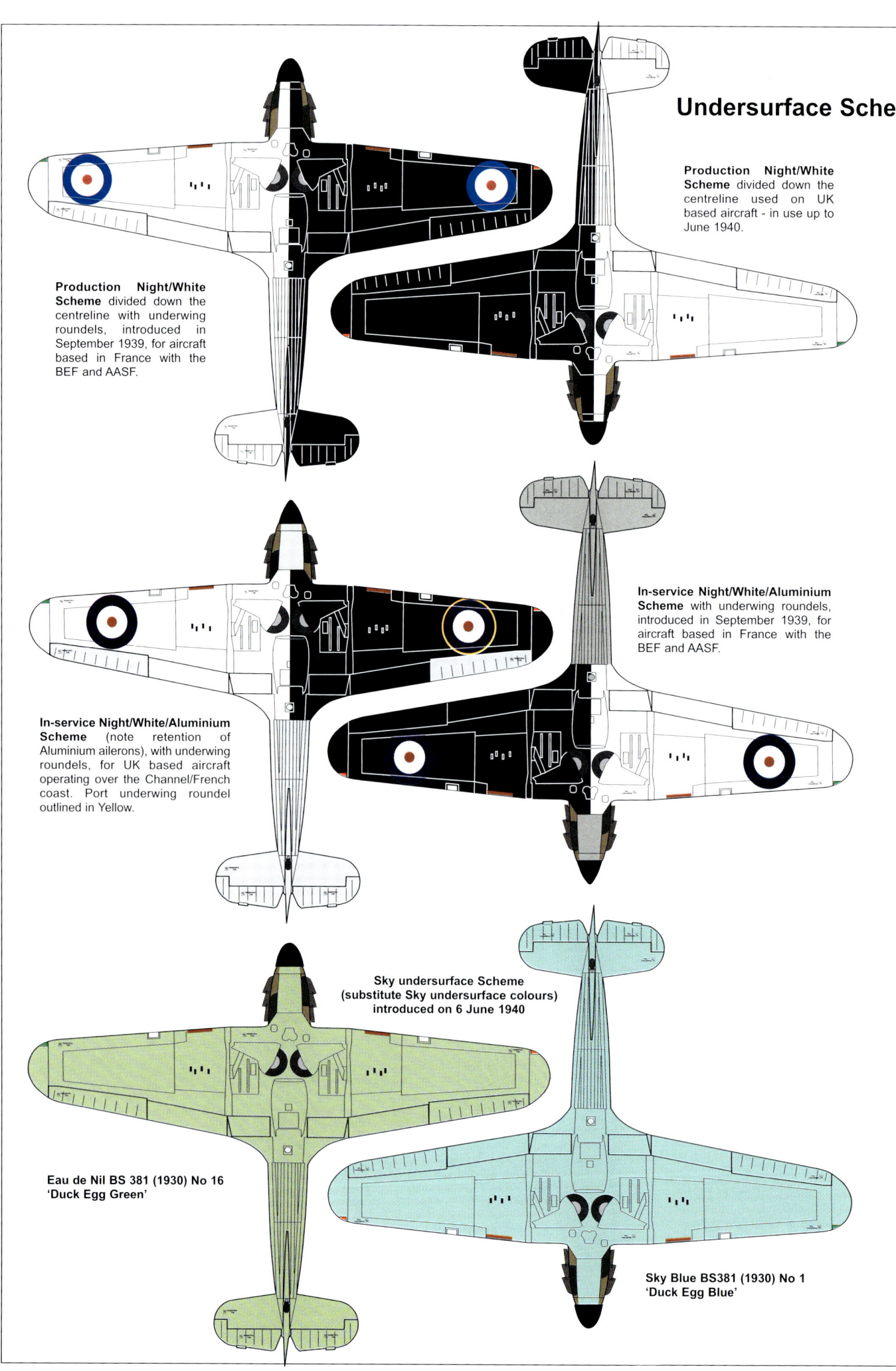

and Markings

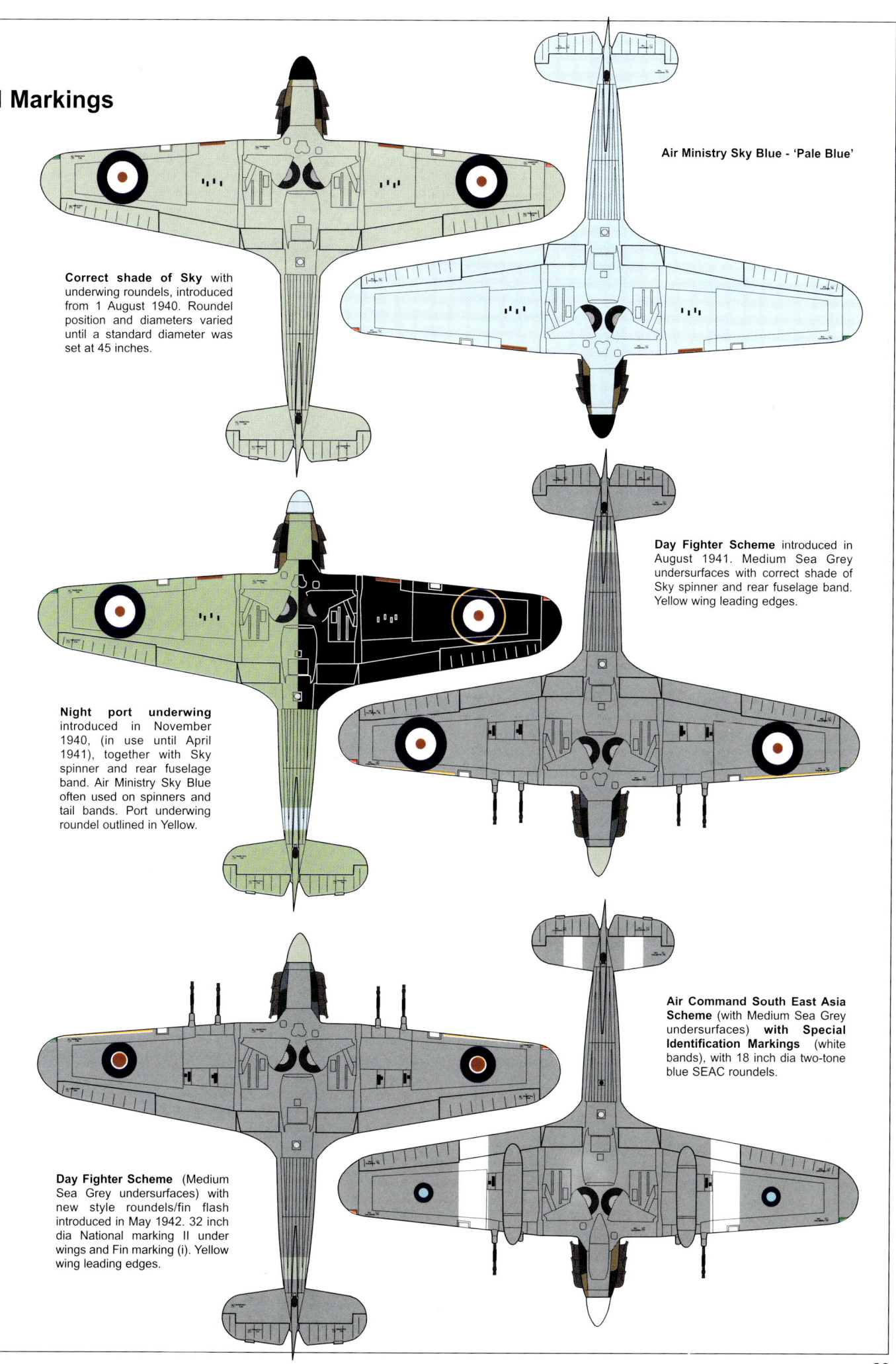

Correct shade of Sky with underwing roundels, introduced from 1 August 1940. Roundel position and diameters varied until a standard diameter was set at 45 inches.

Air Ministry Sky Blue - 'Pale Blue'

Night port underwing introduced in November 1940, (in use until April 1941), together with Sky spinner and rear fuselage band. Air Ministry Sky Blue often used on spinners and tail bands. Port underwing roundel outlined in Yellow.

Day Fighter Scheme introduced in August 1941. Medium Sea Grey undersurfaces with correct shade of Sky spinner and rear fuselage band. Yellow wing leading edges.

Day Fighter Scheme (Medium Sea Grey undersurfaces) with new style roundels/fin flash introduced in May 1942. 32 inch dia National marking II under wings and Fin marking (i). Yellow wing leading edges.

Air Command South East Asia Scheme (with Medium Sea Grey undersurfaces) **with Special Identification Markings** (white bands), with 18 inch dia two-tone blue SEAC roundels.

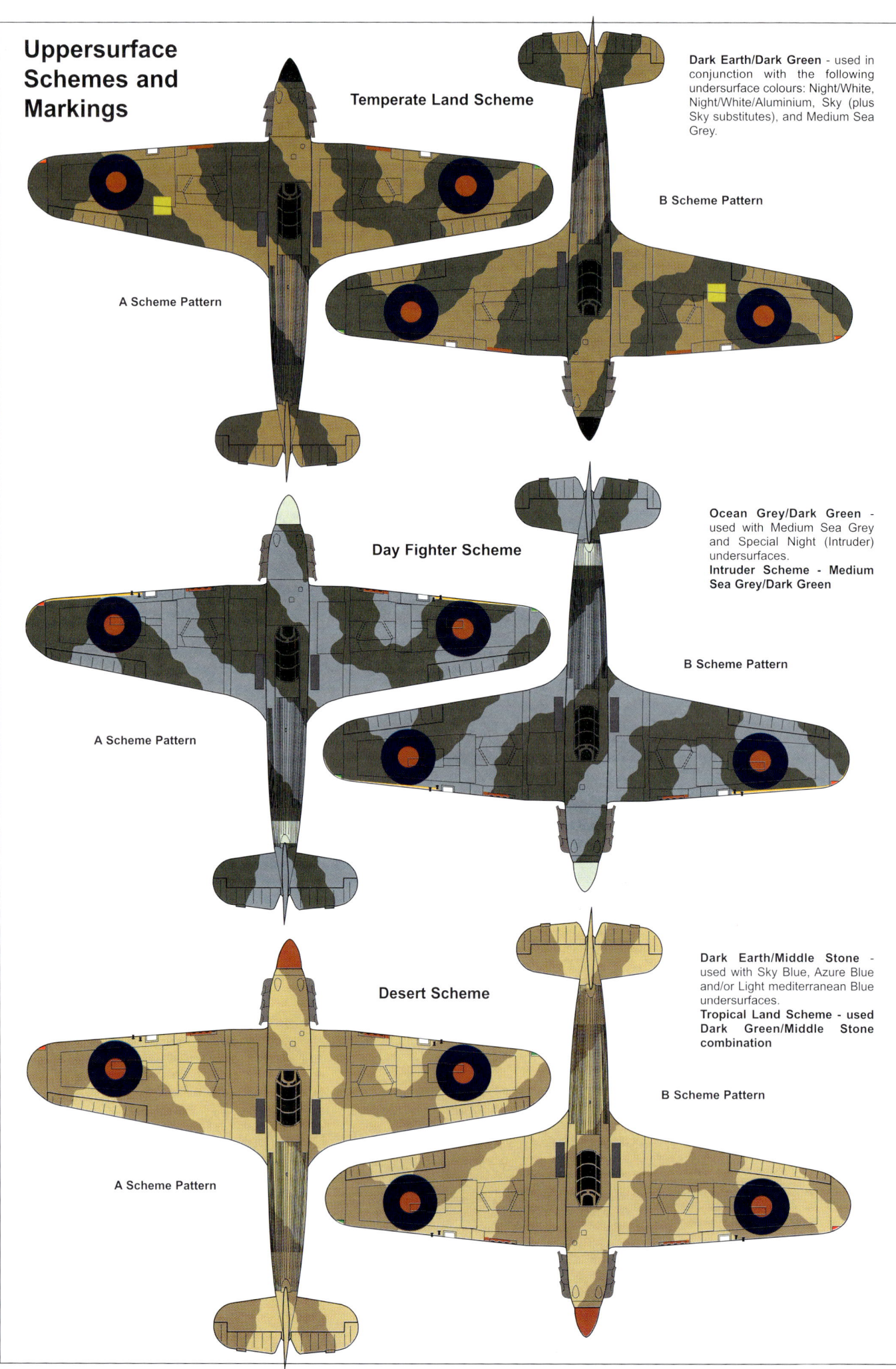

Hurricane Mk I, Z4189, 'L' of 73 Squadron, Malta, 1942
Dark Green and Middle Stone uppersurfaces, in the A Scheme pattern, with Sky Blue undersurfaces. 49 inch Red/Blue upperwing roundels; 35 inch Red/White/Blue/Yellow fuselage roundels, and 50 inch Red/White/Blue underwing roundels. 24 inch x 27 inch fin flash. Red spinner. The Medium Sea Grey code letter is approximately 36 inches high. Note the 'winged bomb' on the emergency breakout panel beneath the canopy.

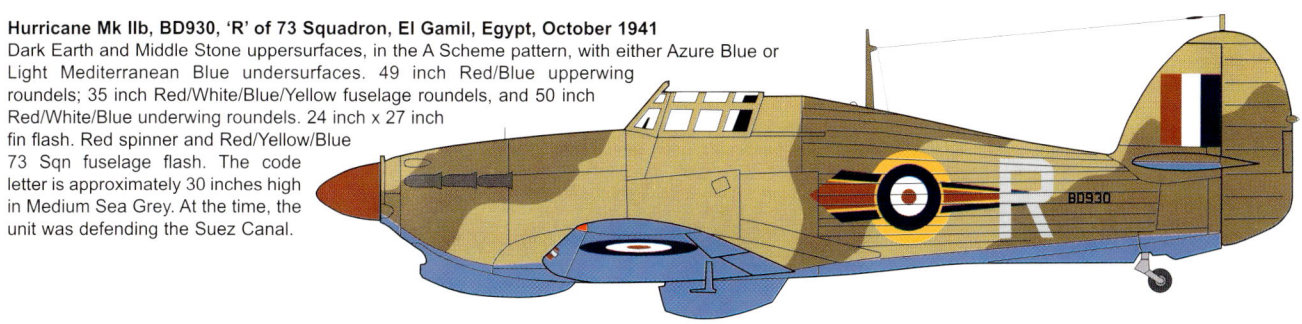

Hurricane Mk IIb, BD930, 'R' of 73 Squadron, El Gamil, Egypt, October 1941
Dark Earth and Middle Stone uppersurfaces, in the A Scheme pattern, with either Azure Blue or Light Mediterranean Blue undersurfaces. 49 inch Red/Blue upperwing roundels; 35 inch Red/White/Blue/Yellow fuselage roundels, and 50 inch Red/White/Blue underwing roundels. 24 inch x 27 inch fin flash. Red spinner and Red/Yellow/Blue 73 Sqn fuselage flash. The code letter is approximately 30 inches high in Medium Sea Grey. At the time, the unit was defending the Suez Canal.

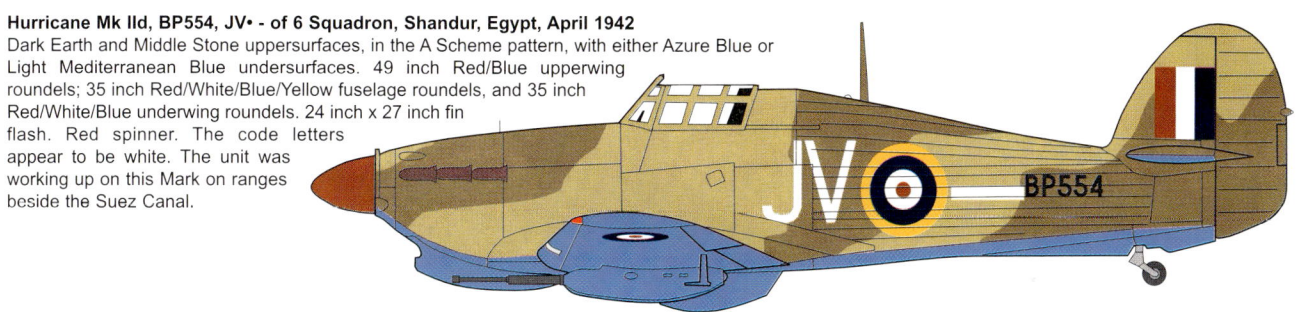

Hurricane Mk IId, BP554, JV• - of 6 Squadron, Shandur, Egypt, April 1942
Dark Earth and Middle Stone uppersurfaces, in the A Scheme pattern, with either Azure Blue or Light Mediterranean Blue undersurfaces. 49 inch Red/Blue upperwing roundels; 35 inch Red/White/Blue/Yellow fuselage roundels, and 35 inch Red/White/Blue underwing roundels. 24 inch x 27 inch fin flash. Red spinner. The code letters appear to be white. The unit was working up on this Mark on ranges beside the Suez Canal.

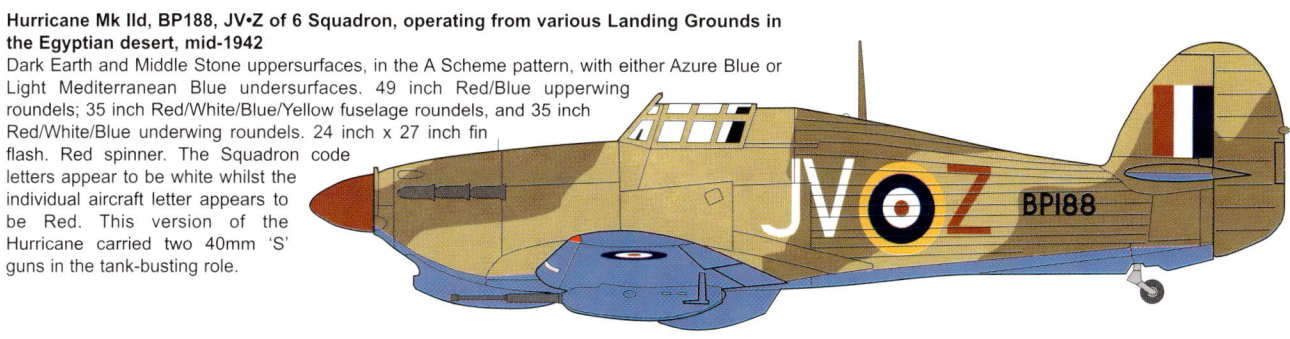

Hurricane Mk IId, BP188, JV•Z of 6 Squadron, operating from various Landing Grounds in the Egyptian desert, mid-1942
Dark Earth and Middle Stone uppersurfaces, in the A Scheme pattern, with either Azure Blue or Light Mediterranean Blue undersurfaces. 49 inch Red/Blue upperwing roundels; 35 inch Red/White/Blue/Yellow fuselage roundels, and 35 inch Red/White/Blue underwing roundels. 24 inch x 27 inch fin flash. Red spinner. The Squadron code letters appear to be white whilst the individual aircraft letter appears to be Red. This version of the Hurricane carried two 40mm 'S' guns in the tank-busting role.

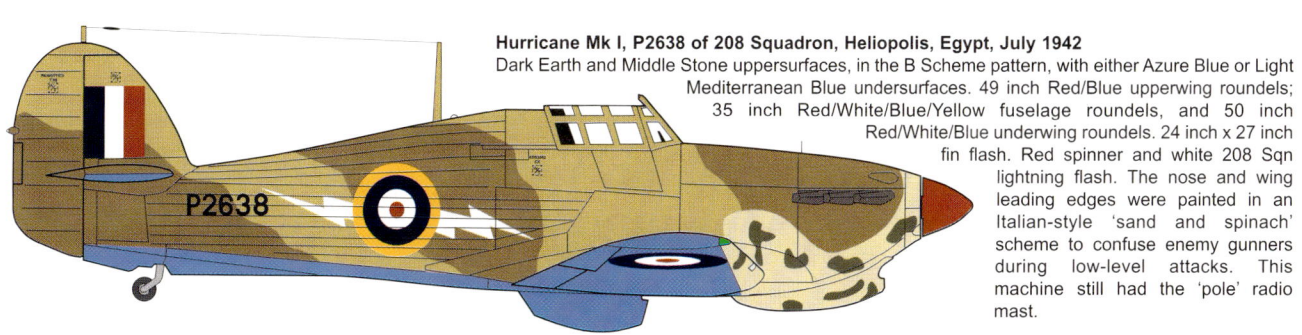

Hurricane Mk I, P2638 of 208 Squadron, Heliopolis, Egypt, July 1942
Dark Earth and Middle Stone uppersurfaces, in the B Scheme pattern, with either Azure Blue or Light Mediterranean Blue undersurfaces. 49 inch Red/Blue upperwing roundels; 35 inch Red/White/Blue/Yellow fuselage roundels, and 50 inch Red/White/Blue underwing roundels. 24 inch x 27 inch fin flash. Red spinner and white 208 Sqn lightning flash. The nose and wing leading edges were painted in an Italian-style 'sand and spinach' scheme to confuse enemy gunners during low-level attacks. This machine still had the 'pole' radio mast.

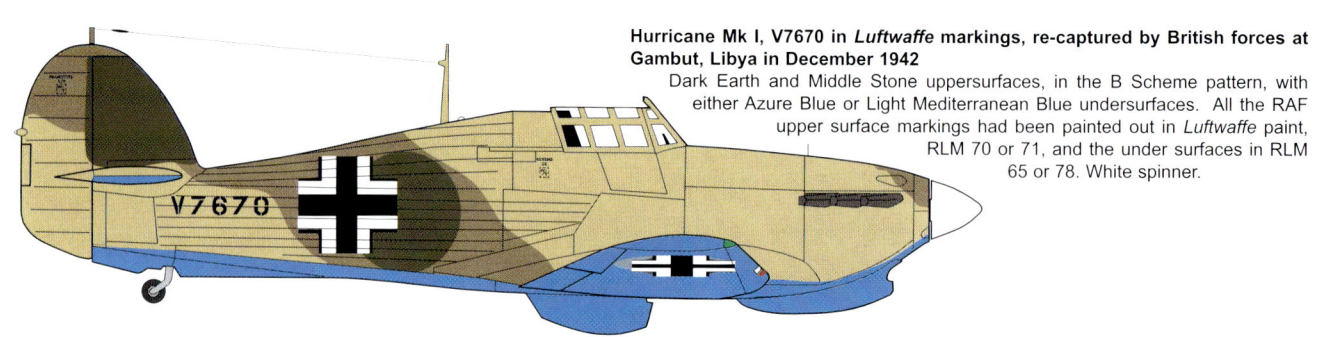

Hurricane Mk I, V7670 in *Luftwaffe* markings, re-captured by British forces at Gambut, Libya in December 1942
Dark Earth and Middle Stone uppersurfaces, in the B Scheme pattern, with either Azure Blue or Light Mediterranean Blue undersurfaces. All the RAF upper surface markings had been painted out in *Luftwaffe* paint, RLM 70 or 71, and the under surfaces in RLM 65 or 78. White spinner.

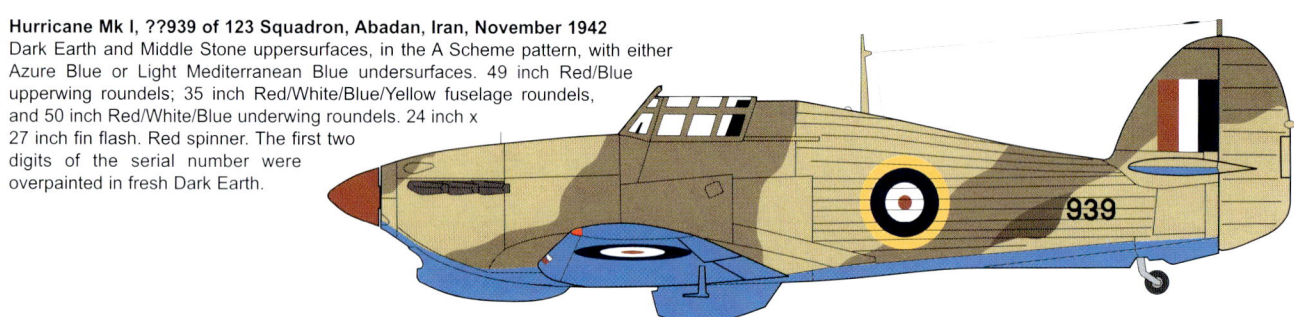

Hurricane Mk I, ??939 of 123 Squadron, Abadan, Iran, November 1942
Dark Earth and Middle Stone uppersurfaces, in the A Scheme pattern, with either Azure Blue or Light Mediterranean Blue undersurfaces. 49 inch Red/Blue upperwing roundels; 35 inch Red/White/Blue/Yellow fuselage roundels, and 50 inch Red/White/Blue underwing roundels. 24 inch x 27 inch fin flash. Red spinner. The first two digits of the serial number were overpainted in fresh Dark Earth.

Hurricane Mk IIb, BD776, WG•F of 128 Squadron, Hastings, Sierra Leone, late 1942
Ocean Grey and Dark Green uppersurfaces, to the A Scheme pattern, with Medium Sea Grey undersurfaces. 49 inch Red/Blue upperwing roundels; 35 inch Red/White/Blue/Yellow fuselage roundels, and 50 inch Red/White/Blue underwing roundels. 24 inch x 30 inch fin flash. Red/White/Blue spinner. Approximately 30 inch Sky codes. This Squadron defended this area of West Africa against incursions from Vichy French forces.

Hurricane Mk IIc, HV817, FT•C of 43 Squadron, Maison Blanche, Algeria, November 1942
Ocean Grey and Dark Green uppersurfaces, to the A Scheme pattern, with Medium Sea Grey undersurfaces. 49 inch Red/Blue National marking I upperwing roundels; 36 inch Red/White/Blue/Yellow National marking III fuselage roundels, and 32 inch National marking II underwing roundels. 24 inch x 24 inch Fin marking (i). Night spinner Approximately 30 inch Sky codes.

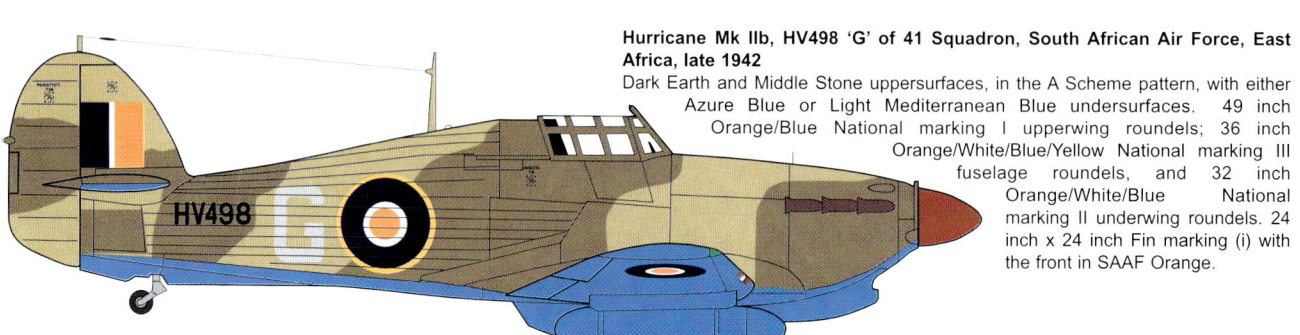

Hurricane Mk IIb, HV498 'G' of 41 Squadron, South African Air Force, East Africa, late 1942
Dark Earth and Middle Stone uppersurfaces, in the A Scheme pattern, with either Azure Blue or Light Mediterranean Blue undersurfaces. 49 inch Orange/Blue National marking I upperwing roundels; 36 inch Orange/White/Blue/Yellow National marking III fuselage roundels, and 32 inch Orange/White/Blue National marking II underwing roundels. 24 inch x 24 inch Fin marking (i) with the front in SAAF Orange.

Hurricane Mk IIb, BP166, KC•J of 238 Squadron, which operated from various bases in Libya and Egypt, 1942
Dark Earth and Middle Stone uppersurfaces, in the A Scheme pattern, with Azure Blue or Light Mediterranean Blue undersurfaces. 49 inch Red/Blue upperwing roundels; 35 inch Red/White/Blue/Yellow fuselage roundels, and 50 inch Red/White/Blue underwing roundels. 24 inch x 27 inch fin flash. Code letters were white approximately 30 inches high. Red spinner. This Squadron was an escort unit for other Hurricane ground attack units.

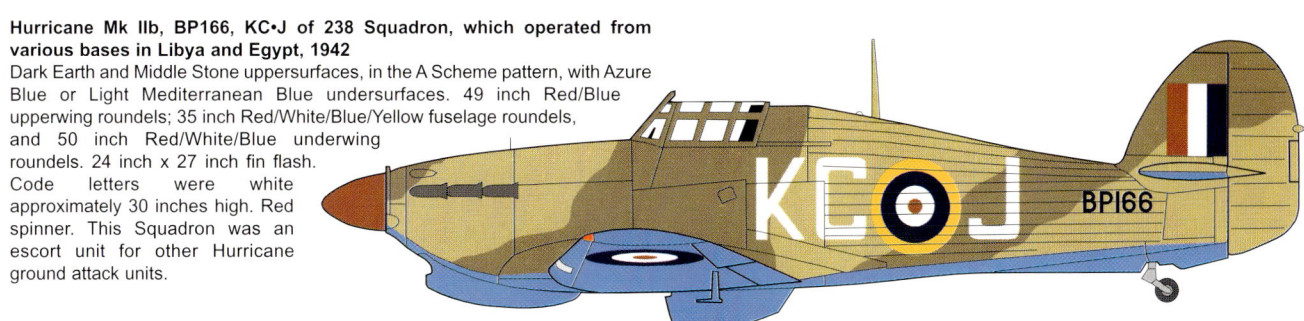

Hurricane Mk IIb, Z4007, FG•S of 335 (Greek) Squadron, Dekheila, Egypt, September 1942
Dark Earth and Middle Stone uppersurfaces, in the A Scheme pattern, with Azure Blue or Light Mediterranean Blue undersurfaces. 49 inch Red/Blue National marking I upperwing roundels; with modified 36 inch Blue/White/Blue/Yellow National marking III fuselage roundels, and 32 inch Blue/White/Blue National marking II underwing roundels. 24 inch x 24 inch Blue/White/Blue Fin marking (i). Red spinner. Code letters were Red with white outline and approximately 24 inches high.

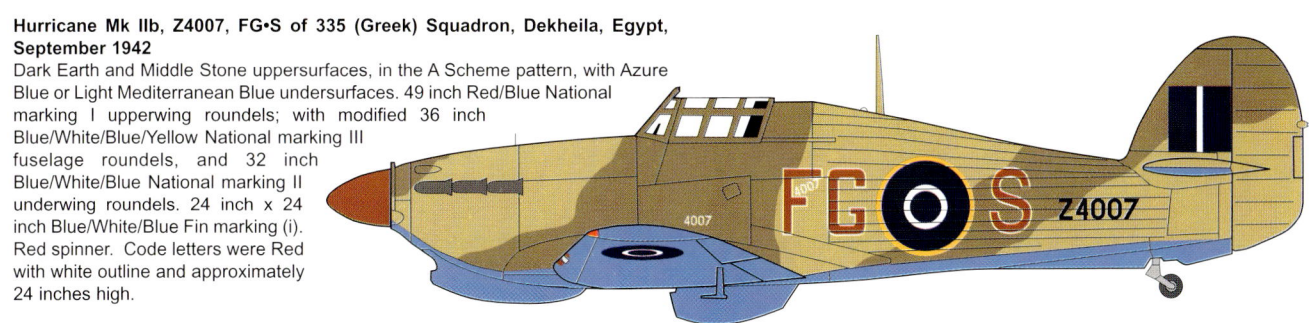

Hurricane Mk IIb, HL887, AK•W of 213 Squadron, which operated from various Landing Grounds in Egypt, 1942
Dark Earth and Middle Stone uppersurfaces, in the A Scheme pattern, with Azure Blue or Light Mediterranean Blue undersurfaces. 49 inch Red/Blue National marking I upperwing roundels; 36 inch Red/White/Blue/Yellow National marking III fuselage roundels, and 32 inch Red/White/Blue National marking II underwing roundels. 24 inch x 24 inch Red/White/Blue Fin marking (i). Red spinner with white back section. Code letters were white and approximately 24 inches high.

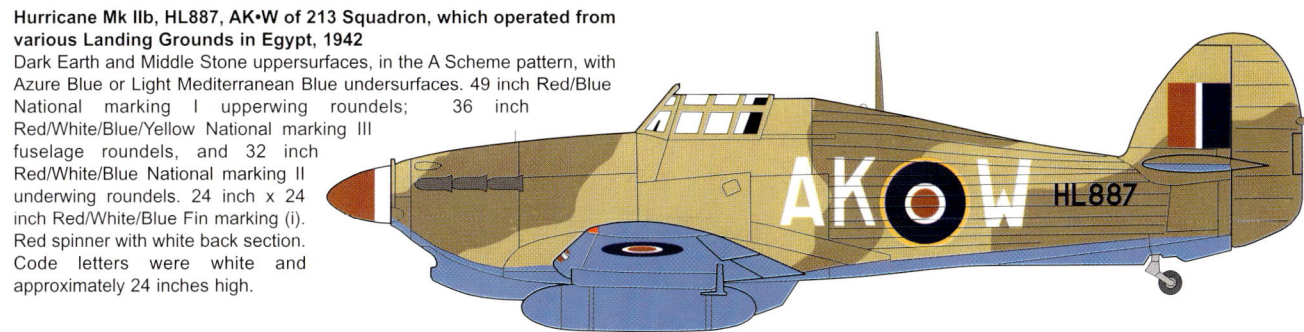

Hurricane Mk IId, HV663 'U' of 6 Squadron, operating from various Landing Grounds in the Egyptian desert, mid 1942
Dark Earth and Middle Stone uppersurfaces, in the A Scheme pattern, with Azure Blue or Light Mediterranean Blue undersurfaces. 49 inch Red/Blue National marking I upperwing roundels; 36 inch Red/White/Blue/Yellow National marking III fuselage roundels, and 32 inch Red/White/Blue National marking II underwing roundels. 24 inch x 24 inch Red/White/Blue Fin marking (i). Red spinner. White code letter, approximately 24 inches high. This version was equipped with two 40mm S guns in the tank-busting role.

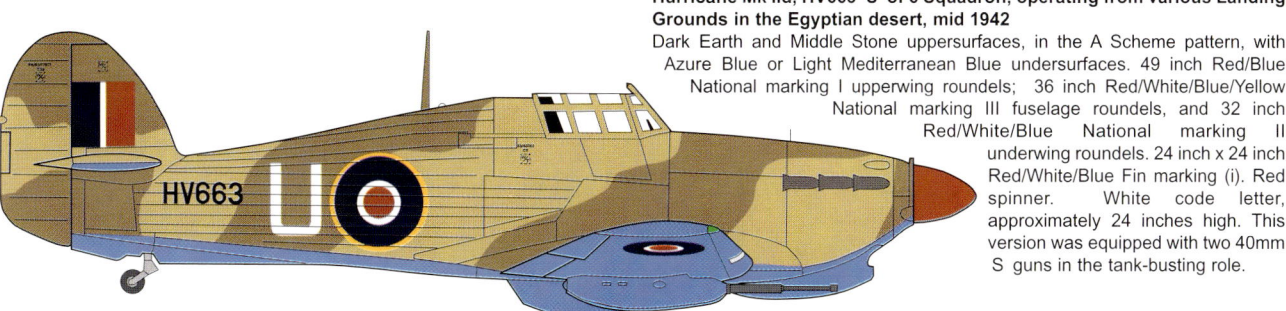

Hurricane Mk IIc, BP389, GO•C of 94 Squadron, El Gamil, Egypt, mid 1942
Dark Earth and Middle Stone uppersurfaces, in the A Scheme pattern, with Azure Blue or Light Mediterranean Blue undersurfaces. 49 inch Red/Blue National marking I upperwing roundels; 36 inch Red/White/Blue/Yellow National marking III fuselage roundels, and 32 inch Red/White/Blue National marking II underwing roundels. 24 inch x 24 inch Red/White/Blue Fin marking (i). Red spinner. White code letters, approximately 24 inches high. Note the darker painted area behind the exhaust manifolds. This unit was tasked with the defence of the Nile Delta region. The outer cannon were removed for performance purposes.

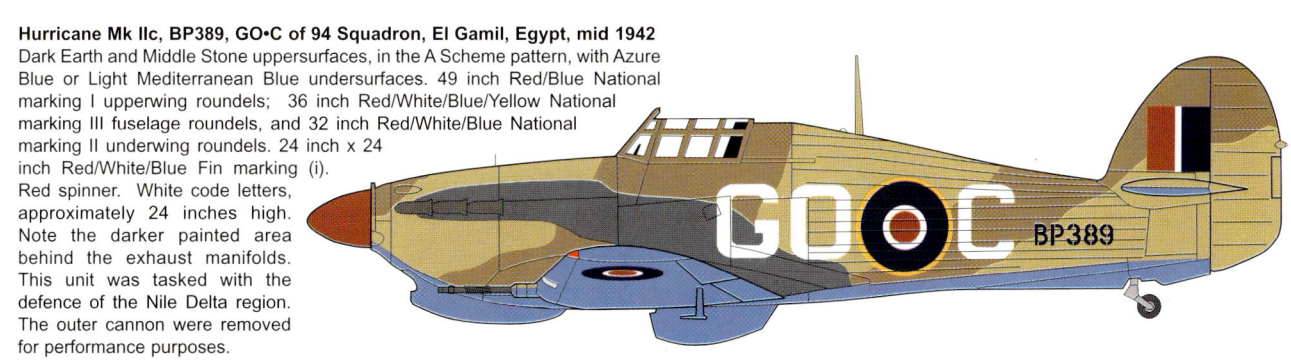

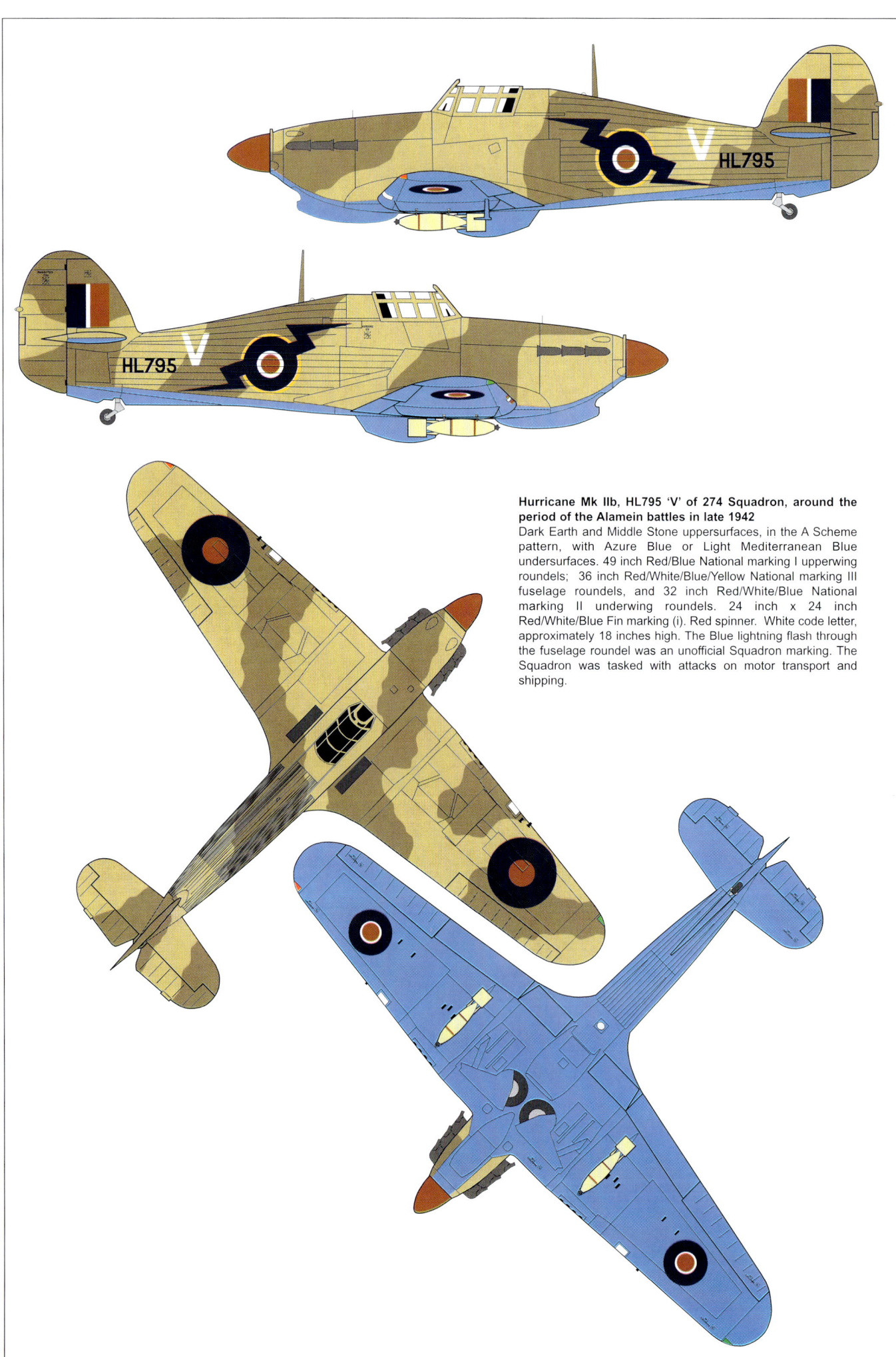

Hurricane Mk IIb, HL795 'V' of 274 Squadron, around the period of the Alamein battles in late 1942

Dark Earth and Middle Stone uppersurfaces, in the A Scheme pattern, with Azure Blue or Light Mediterranean Blue undersurfaces. 49 inch Red/Blue National marking I upperwing roundels; 36 inch Red/White/Blue/Yellow National marking III fuselage roundels, and 32 inch Red/White/Blue National marking II underwing roundels. 24 inch x 24 inch Red/White/Blue Fin marking (i). Red spinner. White code letter, approximately 18 inches high. The Blue lightning flash through the fuselage roundel was an unofficial Squadron marking. The Squadron was tasked with attacks on motor transport and shipping.

Hurricane PR Mk IIc, DG622 of 208 Squadron, El Bassa, Palestine, November 1943
Overall Bosun Blue . 49 inch Red/Blue upperwing roundels. Unit modified 35 inch Red/Blue fuselage roundels. No underwing roundels or fin flash. Black serial number and Red spinner.

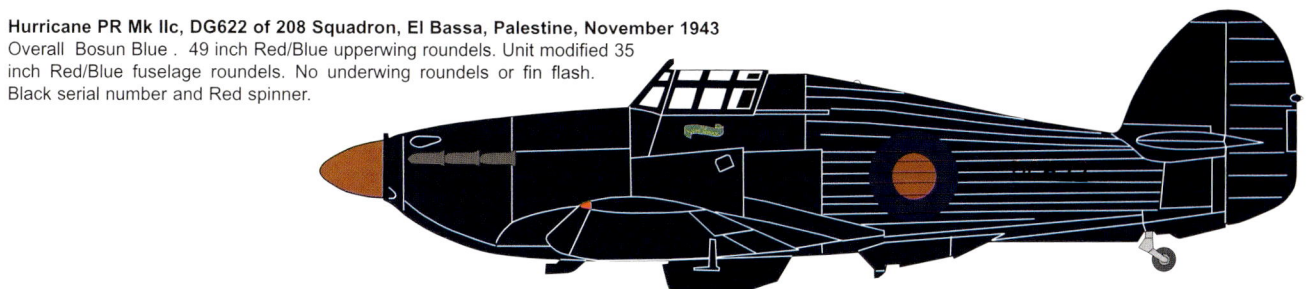

Hurricane PR Mk IIc, HL830 'L' of 208 Squadron, El Bassa, Palestine, November 1943
Overall Bosun Blue . 49 inch Red/Blue upperwing roundels. Unit modified 25 inch Red/Blue fuselage roundels. No underwing roundels or fin flash. Black serial number, Medium blue spinner and individual aircraft letter.

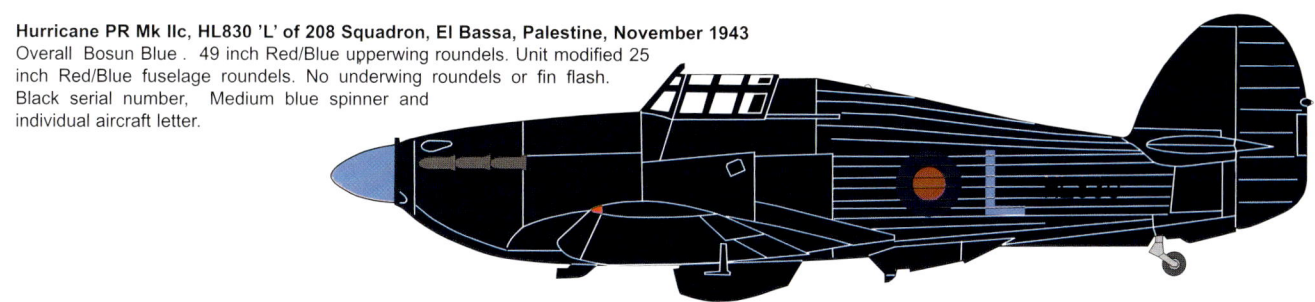

Hurricane Mk I, Z4040 '26' of 71 Operational Training Unit, Ismalia, Egypt, 1943
Dark Earth and Middle Stone uppersurfaces, in the A Scheme pattern, with Azure Blue or Light Mediterranean Blue undersurfaces. 49 inch Red/Blue National marking I upperwing roundels; 36 inch Red/White/Blue/Yellow National marking III fuselage roundels, and 32 inch Red/White/Blue National marking II underwing roundels. 24 inch x 24 inch Red/White/Blue Fin marking (i). Night spinner. Fuselage numerals were white and approximately 24 inches high.

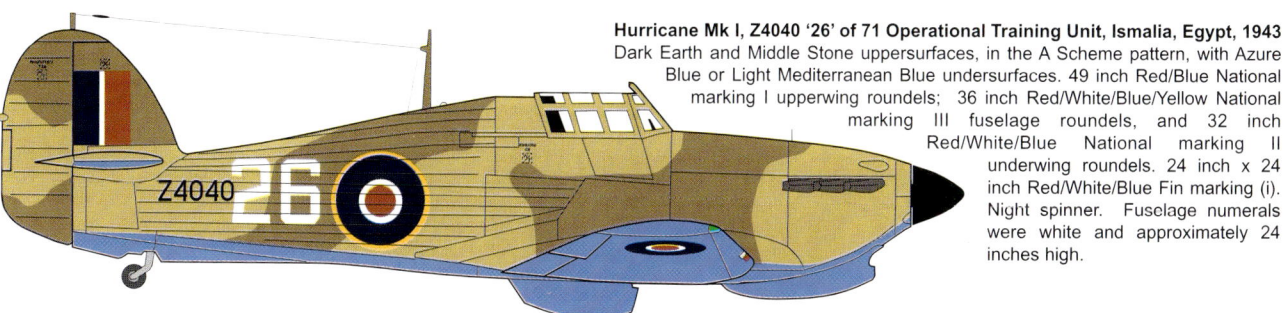

Hurricane Mk IIc, HL973, RZ•G of 241 Squadron, Souk el Khemis, Algeria, October 1943
Dark Earth and Middle Stone uppersurfaces, in the A Scheme pattern, with Azure Blue or Light Mediterranean Blue undersurfaces. 49 inch Red/Blue National marking I upperwing roundels; 36 inch Red/White/Blue/Yellow National marking III fuselage roundels, and 32 inch Red/White/Blue National marking II underwing roundels. 24 inch x 24 inch Red/White/Blue Fin marking (i). Red spinner. Code letters were white and approximately 18 inches high. 69 yellow mission symbols appeared under the cockpit.

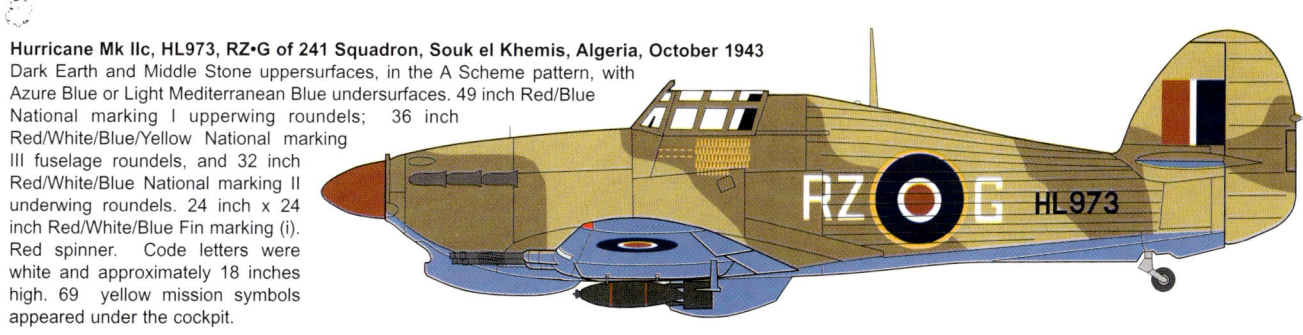

Hurricane Mk IV, KZ609, JV•S of 6 Squadron, RAF Nicosia, Cyprus, 1946
Overall painted Aluminium, with large areas of worn and weathered paintwork. 49 inch Red/White/Blue National marking IA upperwing roundels; 36 inch Red/White/Blue/Yellow National marking III fuselage roundels, and 32 inch Red/White/Blue National marking II underwing roundels. 24 inch x 24 inch Red/White/Blue Fin marking (i). Painted Aluminium spinner. Code letters were Night and approximately 24 inches high.

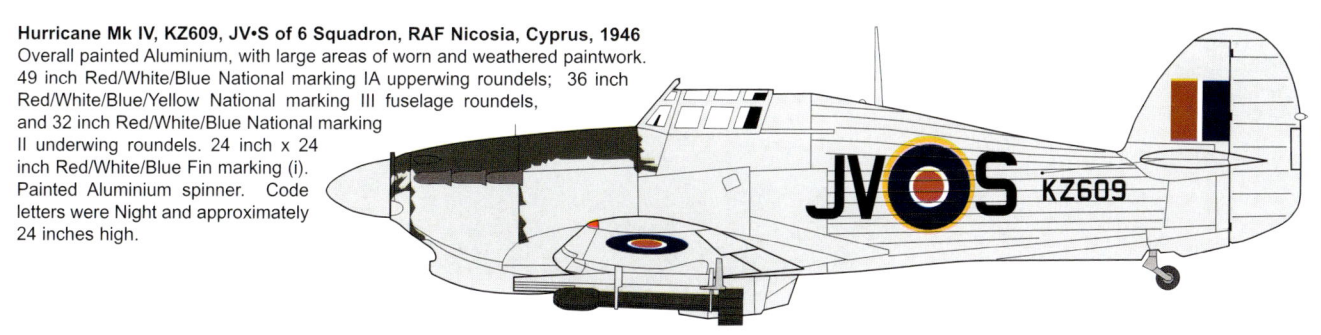

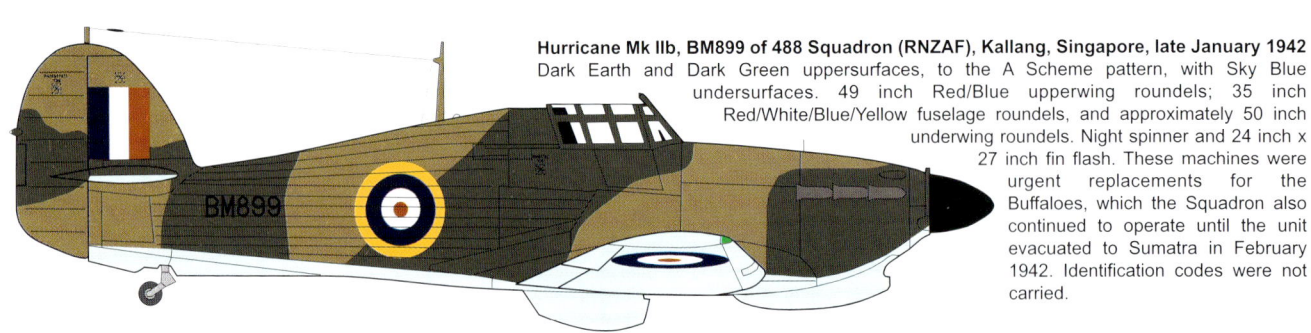

Hurricane Mk IIb, BM899 of 488 Squadron (RNZAF), Kallang, Singapore, late January 1942
Dark Earth and Dark Green uppersurfaces, to the A Scheme pattern, with Sky Blue undersurfaces. 49 inch Red/Blue upperwing roundels; 35 inch Red/White/Blue/Yellow fuselage roundels, and approximately 50 inch underwing roundels. Night spinner and 24 inch x 27 inch fin flash. These machines were urgent replacements for the Buffaloes, which the Squadron also continued to operate until the unit evacuated to Sumatra in February 1942. Identification codes were not carried.

Hurricane Mk IIb, BM904 'F', unit unknown, abandoned at Kallang, Singapore, February 1942
Dark Earth and Dark Green uppersurfaces, to the A Scheme pattern, with Sky Blue undersurfaces. 49 inch Red/Blue upperwing roundels; 35 inch Red/White/Blue/Yellow fuselage roundels, and approximately 50 inch underwing roundels. Night spinner and 24 inch x 27 inch fin flash. White identification letter. This aircraft was subsequently test-flown by the Imperial Japanese Army Air Force.

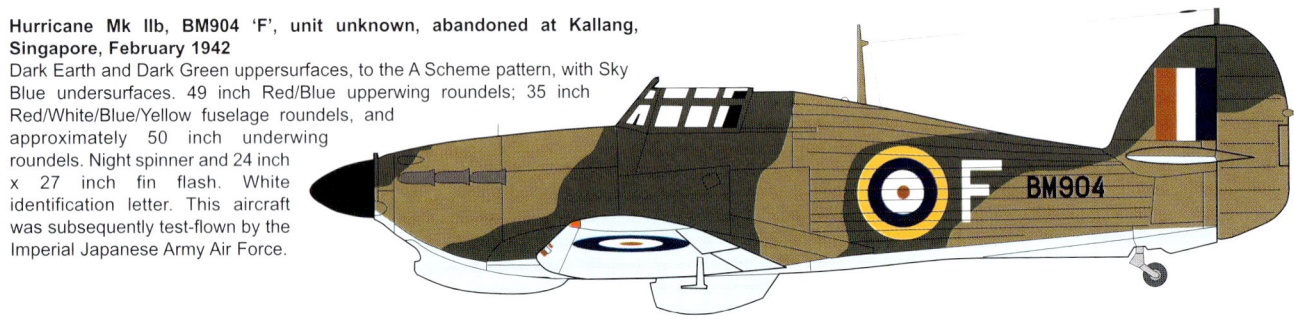

Hurricane Mk IIb, Z5659, WK•C of 135 Squadron, Magwe, Burma, February 1942, flown by P/O J Storey
Dark Earth and Dark Green uppersurfaces, to the A Scheme pattern, with Sky Blue undersurfaces. 49 inch Red/Blue upperwing roundels; 35 inch Red/White/Blue/Yellow fuselage roundels, and approximately 50 inch underwing roundels. Night spinner and 24 inch x 27 inch fin flash. Medium Sea Grey code letters approximately 30 inches high.

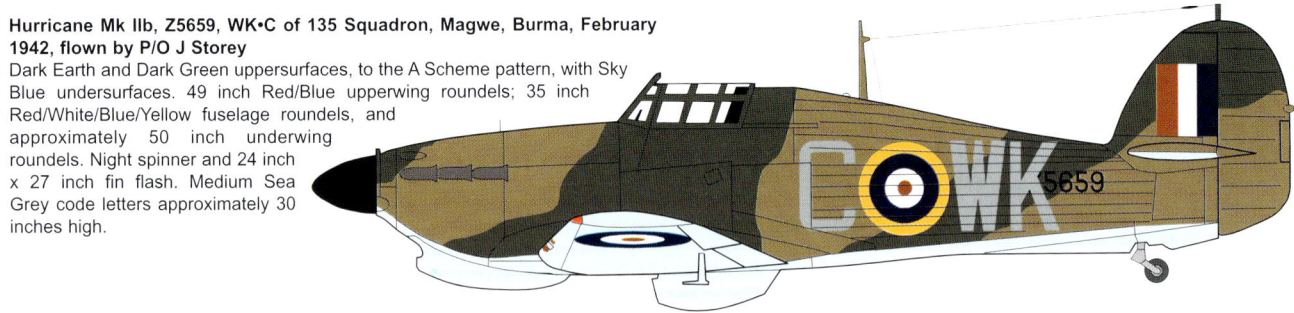

Hurricane Mk IIb, BE322 of 605 Squadron, Tjilitan, Java, February 1942, flown by Sgt J Macintosh
Dark Earth and Dark Green uppersurfaces, to the B Scheme pattern, with Sky Blue undersurfaces. 49 inch Red/Blue upperwing roundels; 35 inch Red/White/Blue/Yellow fuselage roundels, and approximately 50 inch underwing roundels. Red spinner and 24 inch x 27 inch fin flash. Miss Carronvale and Sgt Mac below the cockpit. This machine was previously operated by No 248 Sqn over Java, until its disbandment. No codes carried by either unit.

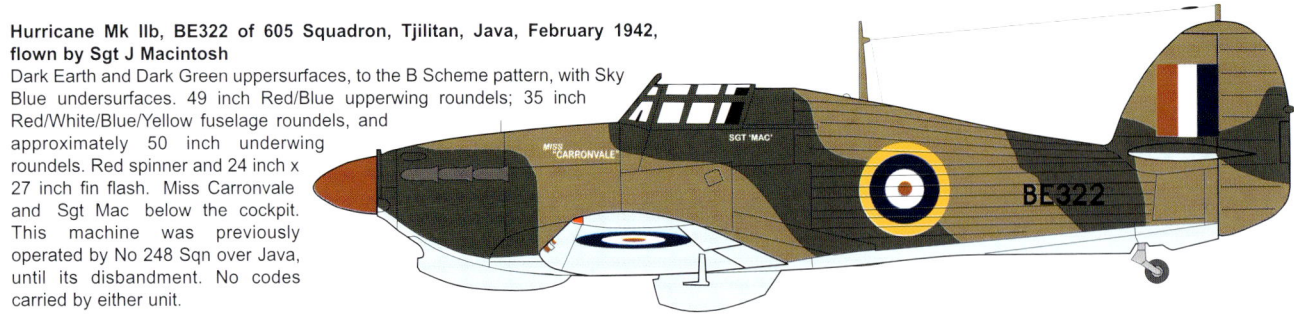

Hurricane Tac R Mk II (FE), BM985 of 28 Squadron, Calcutta, India, mid 1942
Overall Bosun Blue. 49 inch Red/Blue upperwing roundels; 35 inch Red/White/Blue/Yellow fuselage roundels. Night spinner and 24 inch x 27 inch fin flash. No weapons were carried and the radio mast was not fitted.

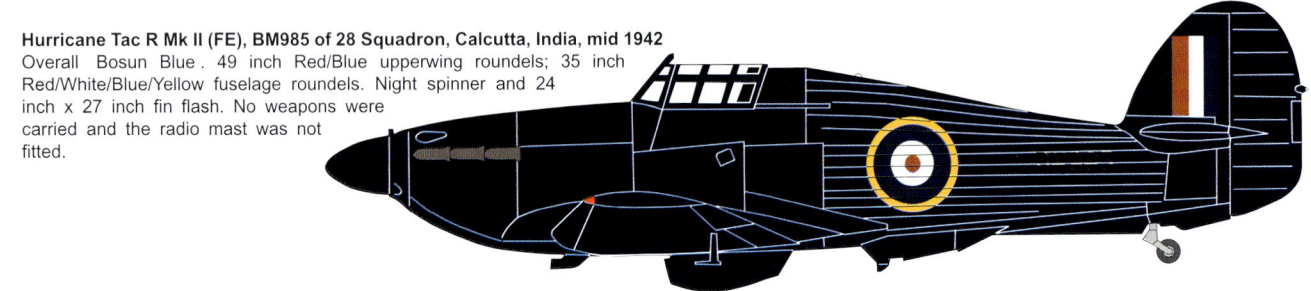

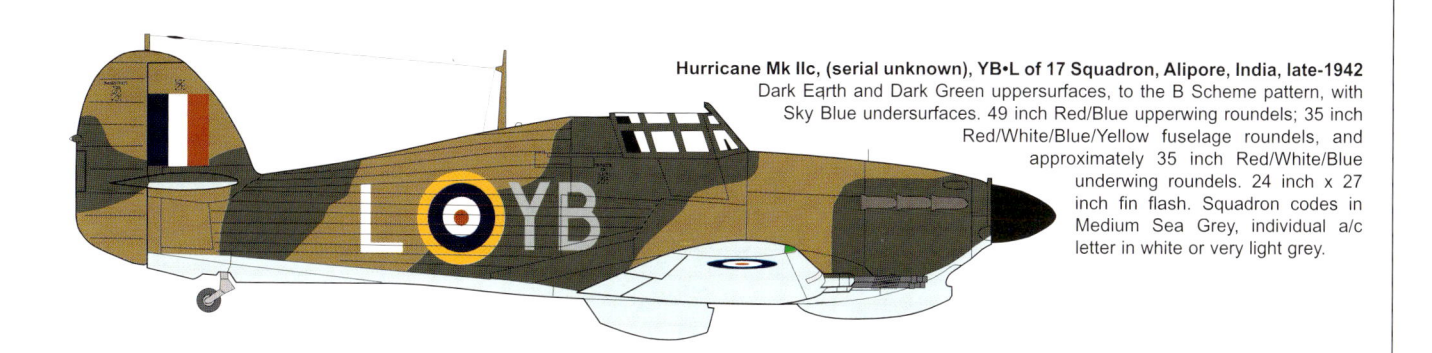

Hurricane Mk IIc, (serial unknown), YB•L of 17 Squadron, Alipore, India, late-1942
Dark Earth and Dark Green uppersurfaces, to the B Scheme pattern, with Sky Blue undersurfaces. 49 inch Red/Blue upperwing roundels; 35 inch Red/White/Blue/Yellow fuselage roundels, and approximately 35 inch Red/White/Blue underwing roundels. 24 inch x 27 inch fin flash. Squadron codes in Medium Sea Grey, individual a/c letter in white or very light grey.

Hurricane PR Mk IIb, BH125 'U' of 3 PRU, Agartala, India, November 1942
Overall Bosun Blue. 49 inch Red/Blue upperwing roundels with 4 inch wide yellow outer rings, and approximately 45 inch Red/White/Blue underwing roundels also with 4 inch wide yellow outer rings. No fuselage roundel was carried. 24 inch x 24 inch Red/Blue fin flash with thin white outline. Night serial number with white approximately 21 inch high code letter. Night spinner.

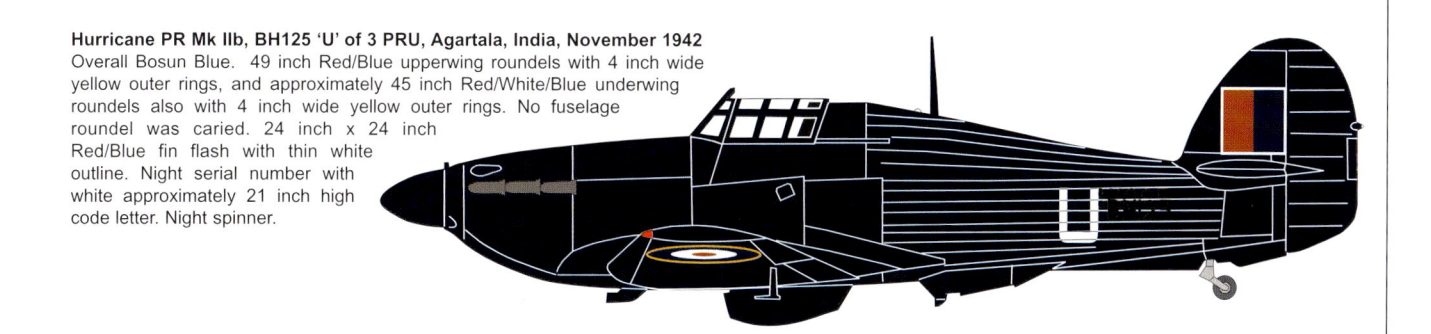

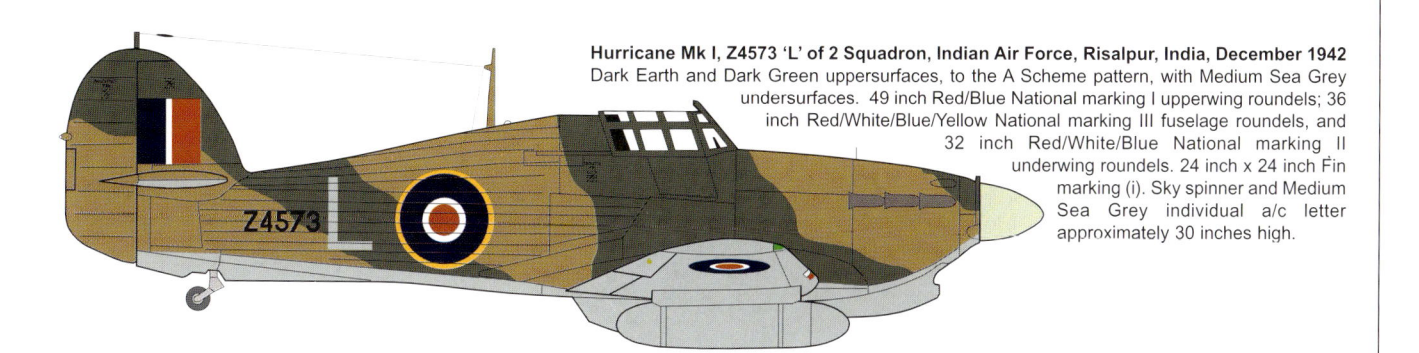

Hurricane Mk I, Z4573 'L' of 2 Squadron, Indian Air Force, Risalpur, India, December 1942
Dark Earth and Dark Green uppersurfaces, to the A Scheme pattern, with Medium Sea Grey undersurfaces. 49 inch Red/Blue National marking I upperwing roundels; 36 inch Red/White/Blue/Yellow National marking III fuselage roundels, and 32 inch Red/White/Blue National marking II underwing roundels. 24 inch x 24 inch Fin marking (i). Sky spinner and Medium Sea Grey individual a/c letter approximately 30 inches high.

Hurricane Mk IIc, BP589, RS•X of 30 Squadron, Dambulla, Ceylon, late 1942
Dark Earth and Middle Stone uppersurfaces, in the A Scheme pattern, with either Azure Blue or Light Mediterranean Blue undersurfaces. 49 inch Red/Blue National marking I upperwing roundels; 36 inch Red/White/Blue/Yellow National marking III fuselage roundels, and 32 inch Red/White/Blue National marking II underwing roundels. 18 inch x 30 inch modified Fin marking (i). Night code letters. Red spinner.

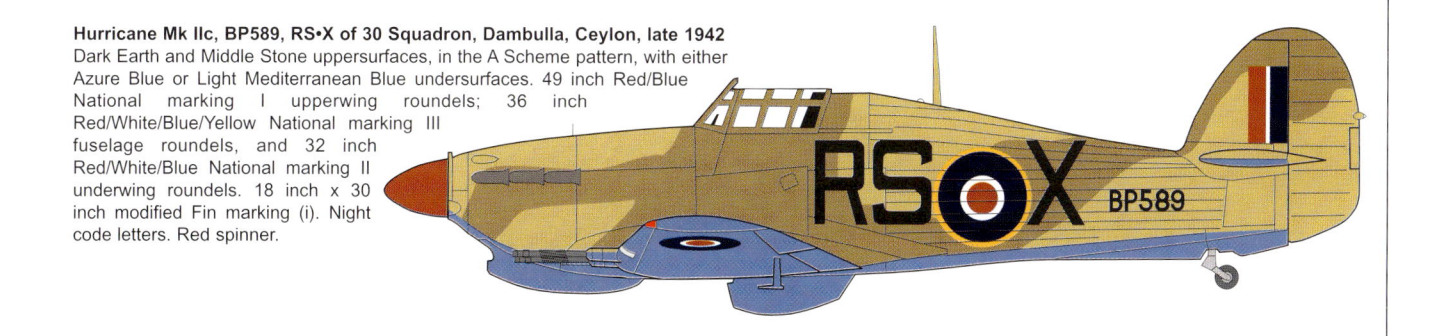

Hurricane Mk IIb, BG802 of 28 Squadron, Cox's Bazaar, India, 1943
Dark Earth and Dark Green uppersurfaces, to the A Scheme pattern, with Sky undersurfaces. 49 inch Red/Blue National marking I upperwing roundels; 36 inch Red/White/Blue/Yellow National marking III fuselage roundels, and 32 inch Red/White/Blue National marking II underwing roundels. 6 inch x 30 inch modified Fin marking (i). Night spinner. Note natural metal replacement panel. This Squadron flew tactical reconnaissance missions for the Army throughout the campaign in Burma, hence the panels protecting the camera lenses from leaking engine oil and the fixed 44 gallon fuel tanks.

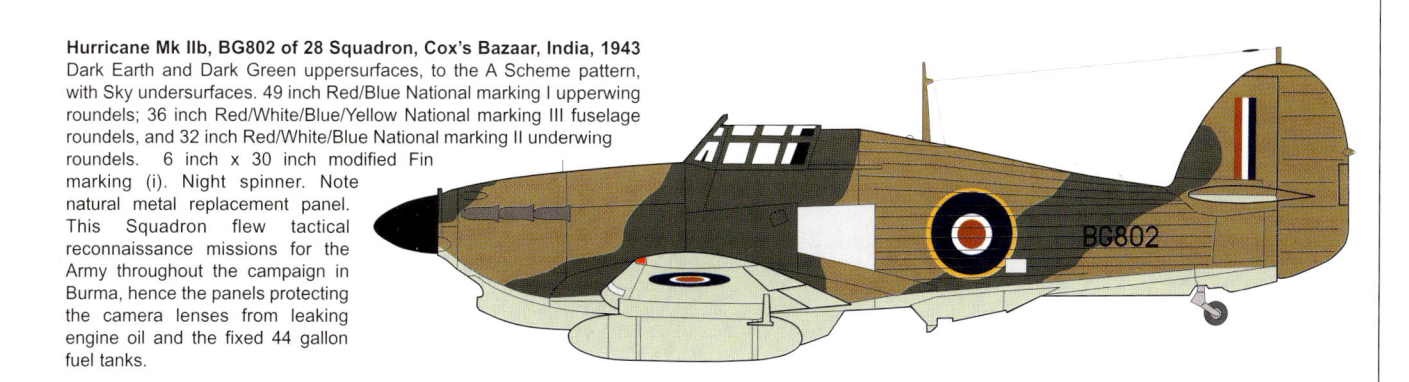

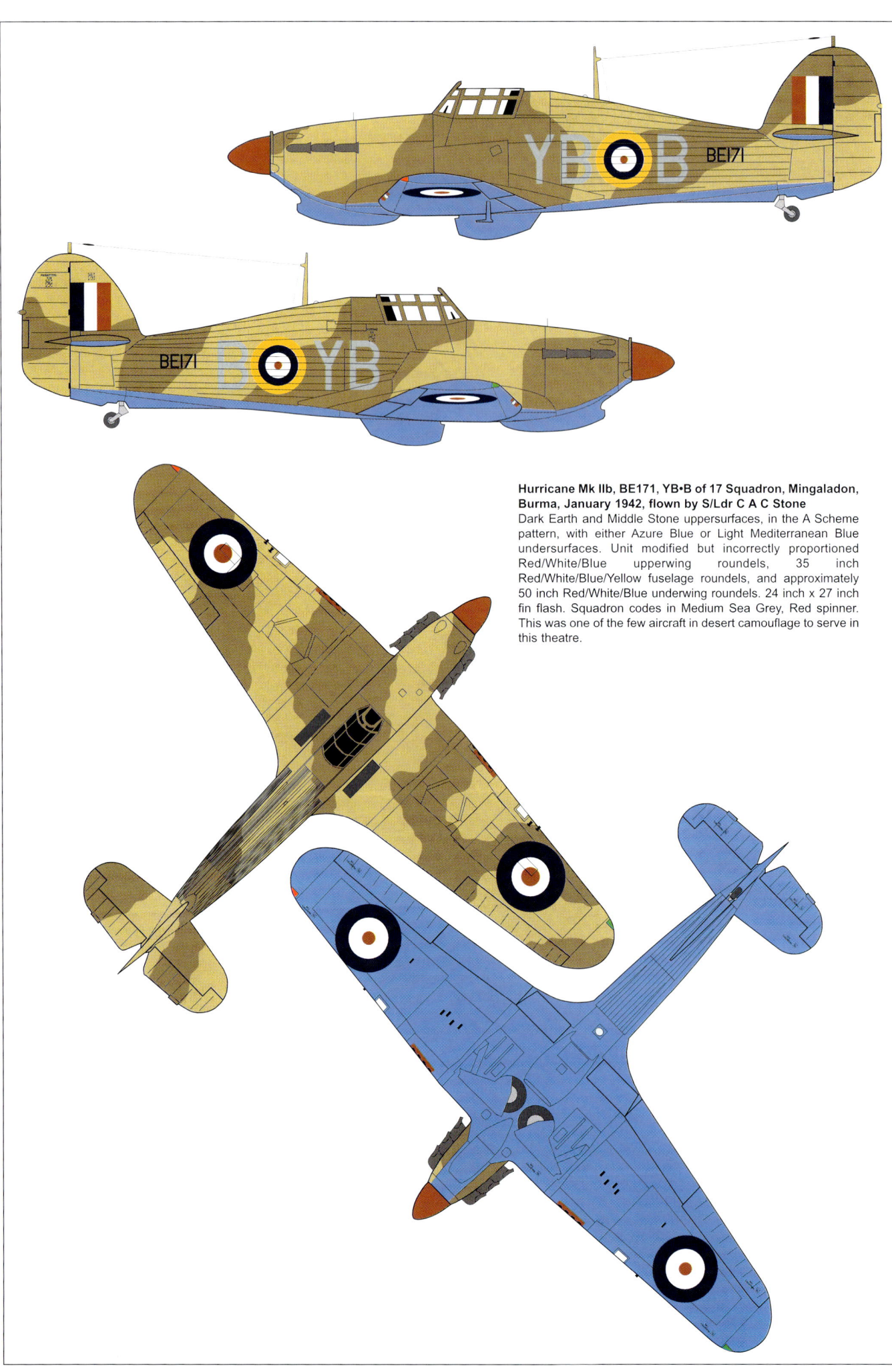

Hurricane Mk IIb, BE171, YB•B of 17 Squadron, Mingaladon, Burma, January 1942, flown by S/Ldr C A C Stone

Dark Earth and Middle Stone uppersurfaces, in the A Scheme pattern, with either Azure Blue or Light Mediterranean Blue undersurfaces. Unit modified but incorrectly proportioned Red/White/Blue upperwing roundels, 35 inch Red/White/Blue/Yellow fuselage roundels, and approximately 50 inch Red/White/Blue underwing roundels. 24 inch x 27 inch fin flash. Squadron codes in Medium Sea Grey, Red spinner. This was one of the few aircraft in desert camouflage to serve in this theatre.

Hurricane Mk IIc, LE336 'F' of 34 Squadron, Palel, India, late-1943
Dark Earth and Dark Green uppersurfaces in an in-service repaint pattern similar to the A Scheme pattern, with non-standard Azure Blue or Light Mediterranean Blue undersurfaces. 18 inch dia India White (pale blue)/Blue roundels in six positions with India White/Blue 18 inch x 24 inch fin flash. Approximately 24 inch high white code letter and India White (pale plue) spinner. This unit was tasked with Rhubarb operations.

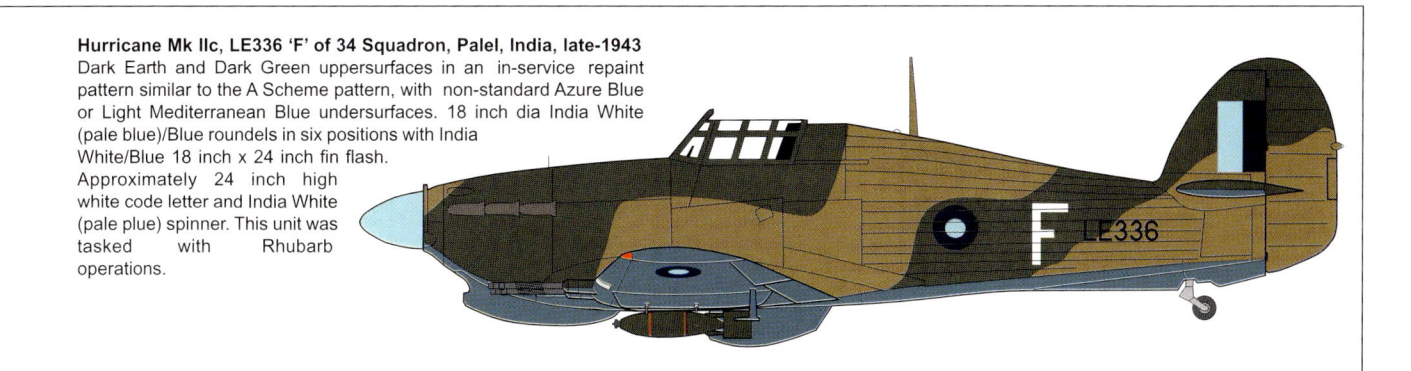

Hurricane Mk IIc, KZ371 'R' of 1 Squadron, Indian Air Force, Miranshah, India, late 1943
Ocean Grey and Dark Green uppersurfaces in the A Scheme pattern with Medium Sea Grey undersides. 18 inch dia India White/Blue roundels in six positions with India White/Blue 18 inch x 24 inch fin flash. Sky spinner and rear fuselage tail band. Approximately 30 inch high Medium Sea Grey code letter. This was one of the few training machines that retained Yellow wing leading edge stripes.

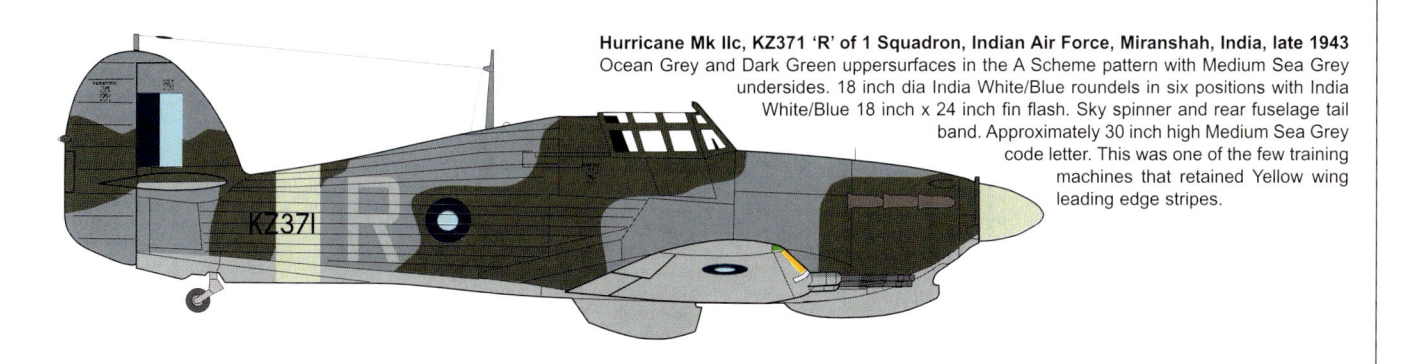

Hurricane Mk IIb, BD701, ZT•M of 258 Squadron, Racecourse, Ceylon, January 1943
Dark Earth and Dark Green uppersurfaces in the A Scheme pattern, with non-standard Sky Blue undersurfaces. 18 inch dia India White/Blue roundels in six positions with India White/Blue 18 inch x 24 inch fin flash. Approximately 24 inch high white code letters and Red spinner.

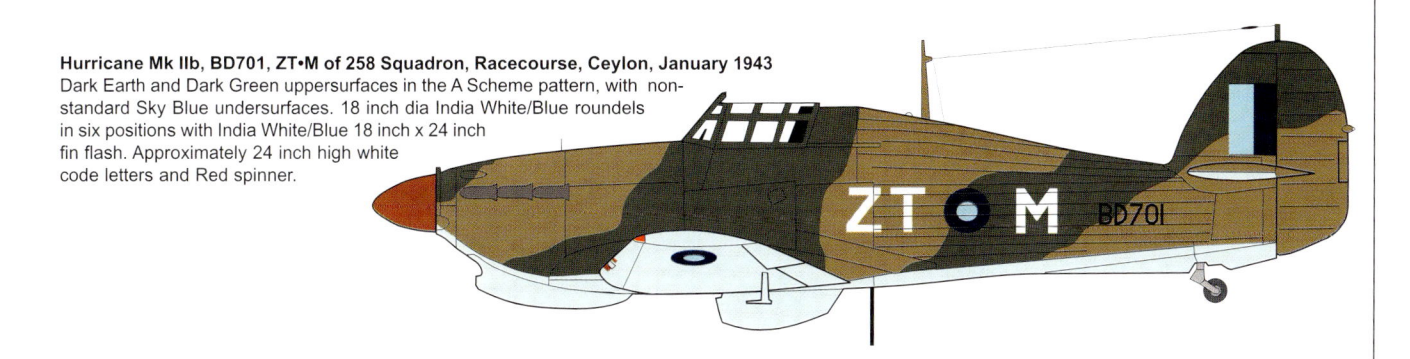

Hurricane Mk IIc, KZ352, A•A of 1 Squadron, Indian Air Force, Imphal, Burma, 1944
Ocean Grey and Dark Green uppersurfaces in the A Scheme pattern with Medium Sea Grey undersides. 18 inch dia India White/Blue roundels in six positions with India White/Blue 18 inch x 24 inch fin flash. Air Command South East Asia Special Identification Markings on mainplanes, tailplanes and fin, with White spinner. Approximately 24 inch high white code letters. Note Assam Elephant marking under cockpit.

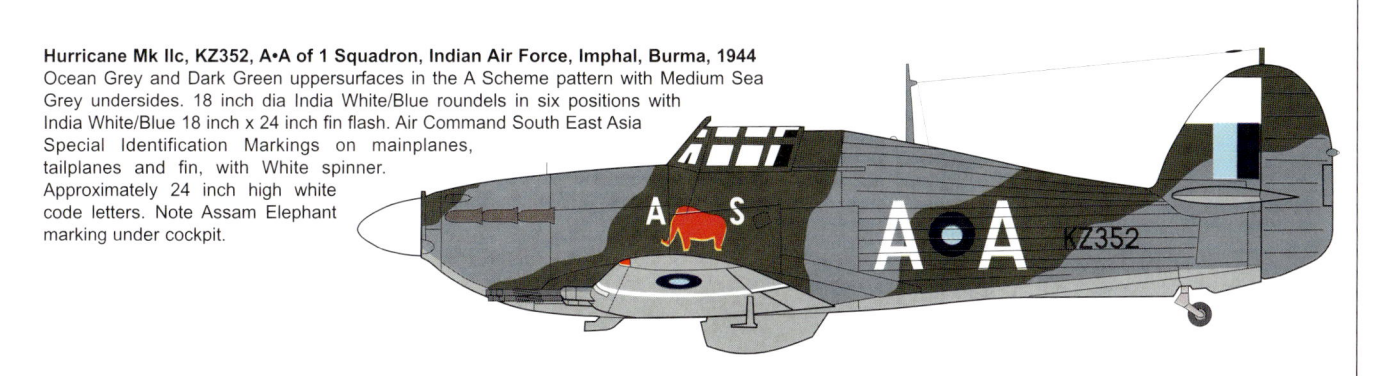

Hurricane Mk IV, KX802, AW•B of 42 Squadron, Onbauk, Burma, 1944
Dark Earth and Dark Green uppersurfaces in the A Scheme pattern, with Medium Sea Grey undersurfaces. 18 inch dia India White/Blue roundels in six positions with India White/Blue 18 inch x 24 inch fin flash. Approximately 18 inch high white code letters and India White spinner. Used for Rhubarb operations.

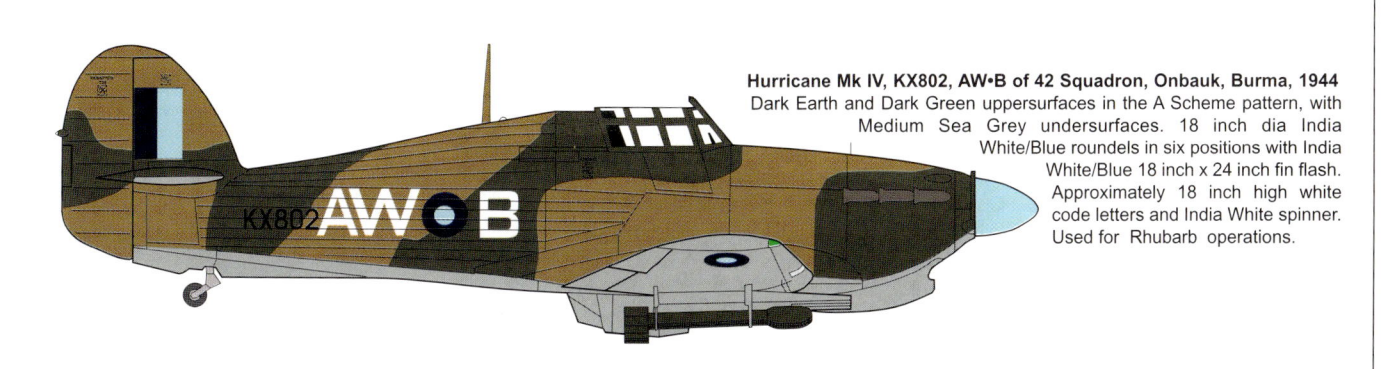

Hurricane Mk IIc, LE146 of 2 Squadron, Indian Air Force, Akyab, Burma, 1945
Ocean Grey and Dark Green uppersurfaces in the A Scheme pattern with Medium Sea Grey undersides. 18 inch dia India White/Blue roundels in six positions with India White/Blue 18 inch x 21 inch fin flash. Air Command South East Asia Special Identification Markings on mainplanes, tailplanes and fin, with White spinner. Note the Special Identification Marking across fin *and* rudder, and bird/moon artwork on nose.

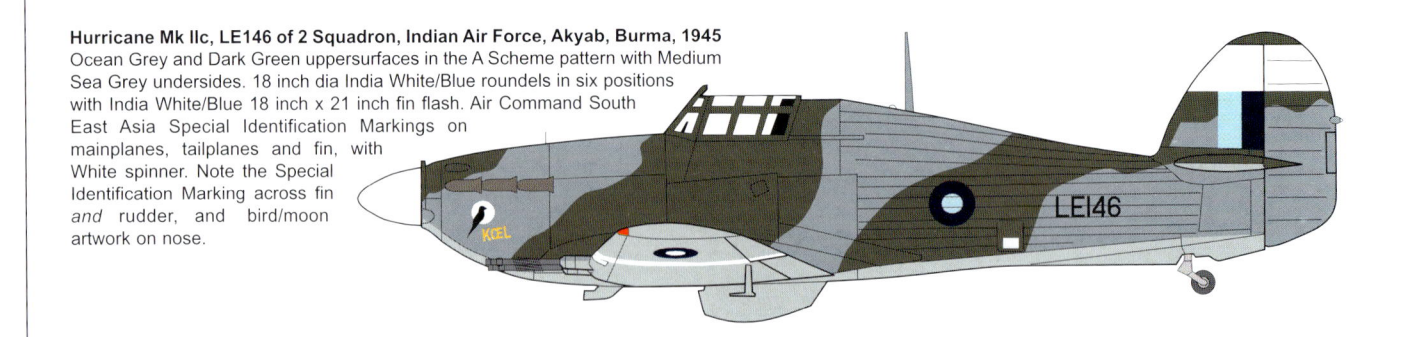

Hurricane Mk IIc, LB836 'L' of 34 Squadron, Cox's Bazaar, Burma 1945
Ocean Grey and Dark Green uppersurfaces in the A Scheme pattern with Medium Sea Grey undersides. 18 inch dia India White/Blue roundels in six positions with India White/Blue 18 inch x 24 inch fin flash. Approximately 30 inch Medium Sea Grey code letter and Night spinner.

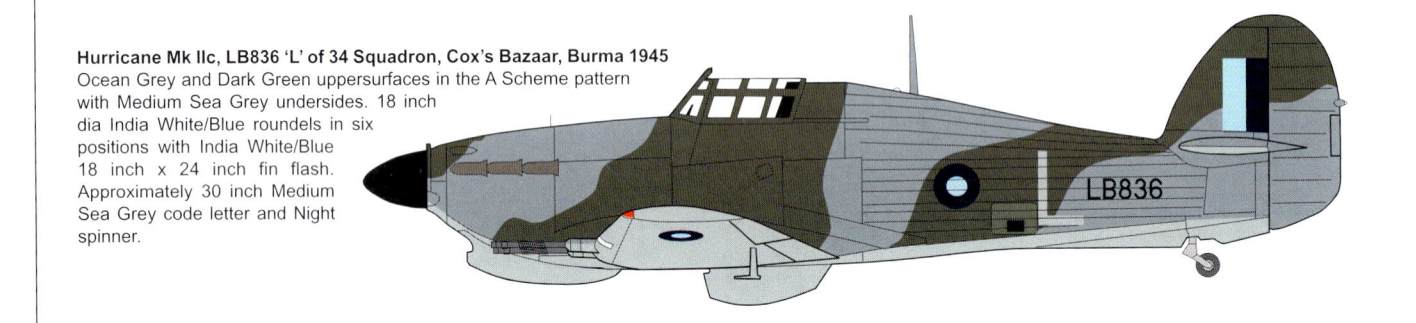

Hurricane FR Mk IIc, LD903 'N' of 10 Squadron, Indian Air Force, Kyaukpyu, Burma, April 1945
Ocean Grey and Dark Green uppersurfaces in the A Scheme pattern with Medium Sea Grey undersides. 18 inch dia India White/Blue roundels in six positions with India White/Blue 18 inch wide fin flash truncated by Special Identification Marking. Air Command South East Asia Special Identification Markings on mainplanes, tailplanes and across fin *and* rudder. White spinner. Approximately 21 inch white code letter and India White spinner.

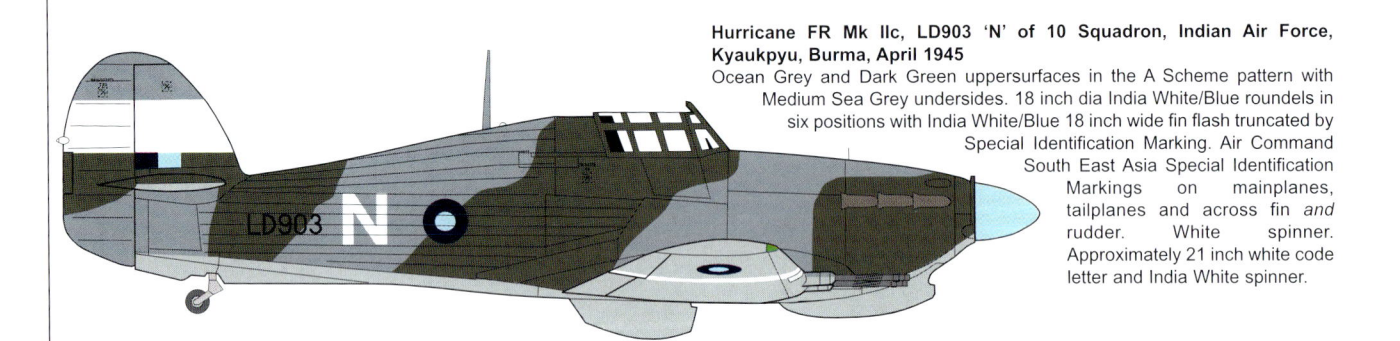

Hurricane Mk IV, KZ944 'S' of 43 Squadron, Meiktila, Burma, July 1945
Overall painted Aluminium with 18 inch dia India White/Blue roundels in six positions and India White/Blue 18 inch x 24 inch fin flash. Approximately 24 inch high Night code letter and Night spinner. This machine was the unit's communications hack.

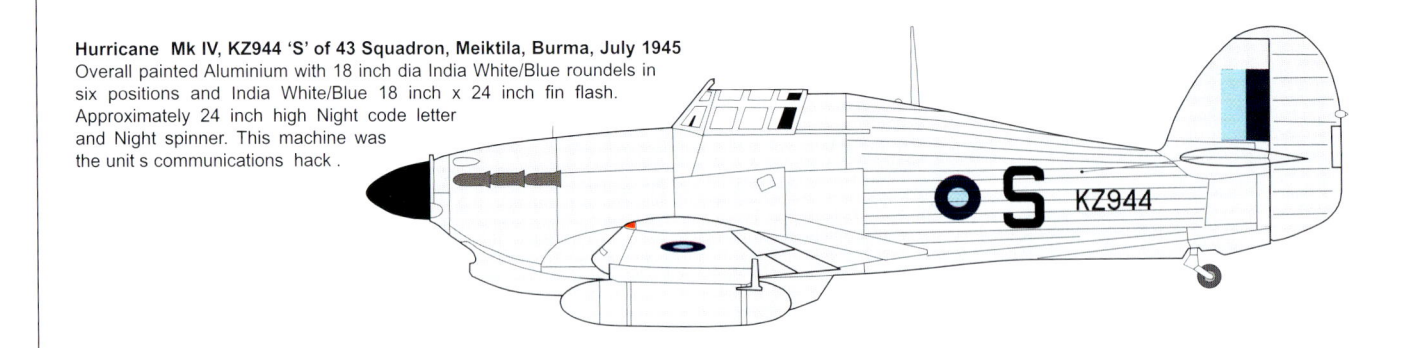

Hurricane Mk IV, KZ248 of 28 Squadron, Kuala Lumpar, Malaya, 1946
Dark Earth and Dark Green uppersurfaces in the B Scheme pattern, with Medium Sea Grey undersurfaces. 18 inch dia India White/Blue roundels in six positions with India White/Blue 18 inch x 24 inch fin flash. Note serial number repeated in white approx 6 inches high on fin top. Sky spinner.

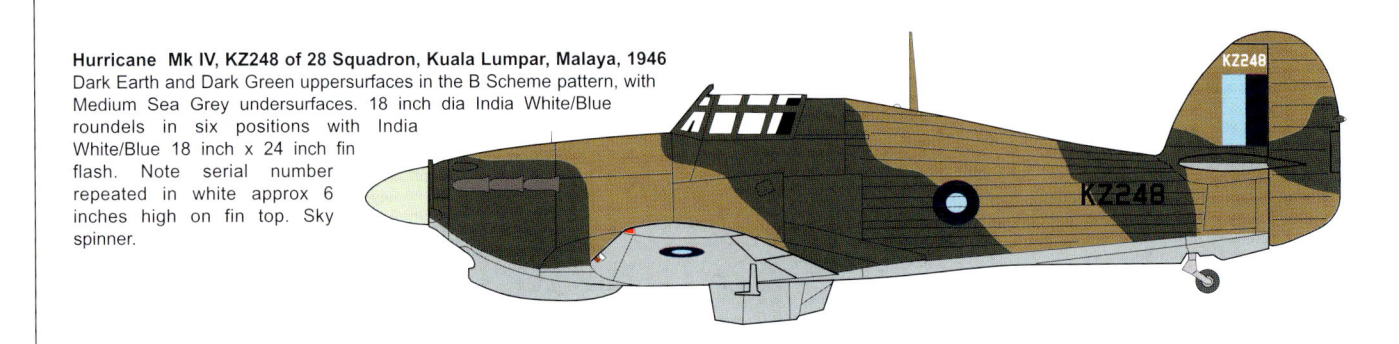

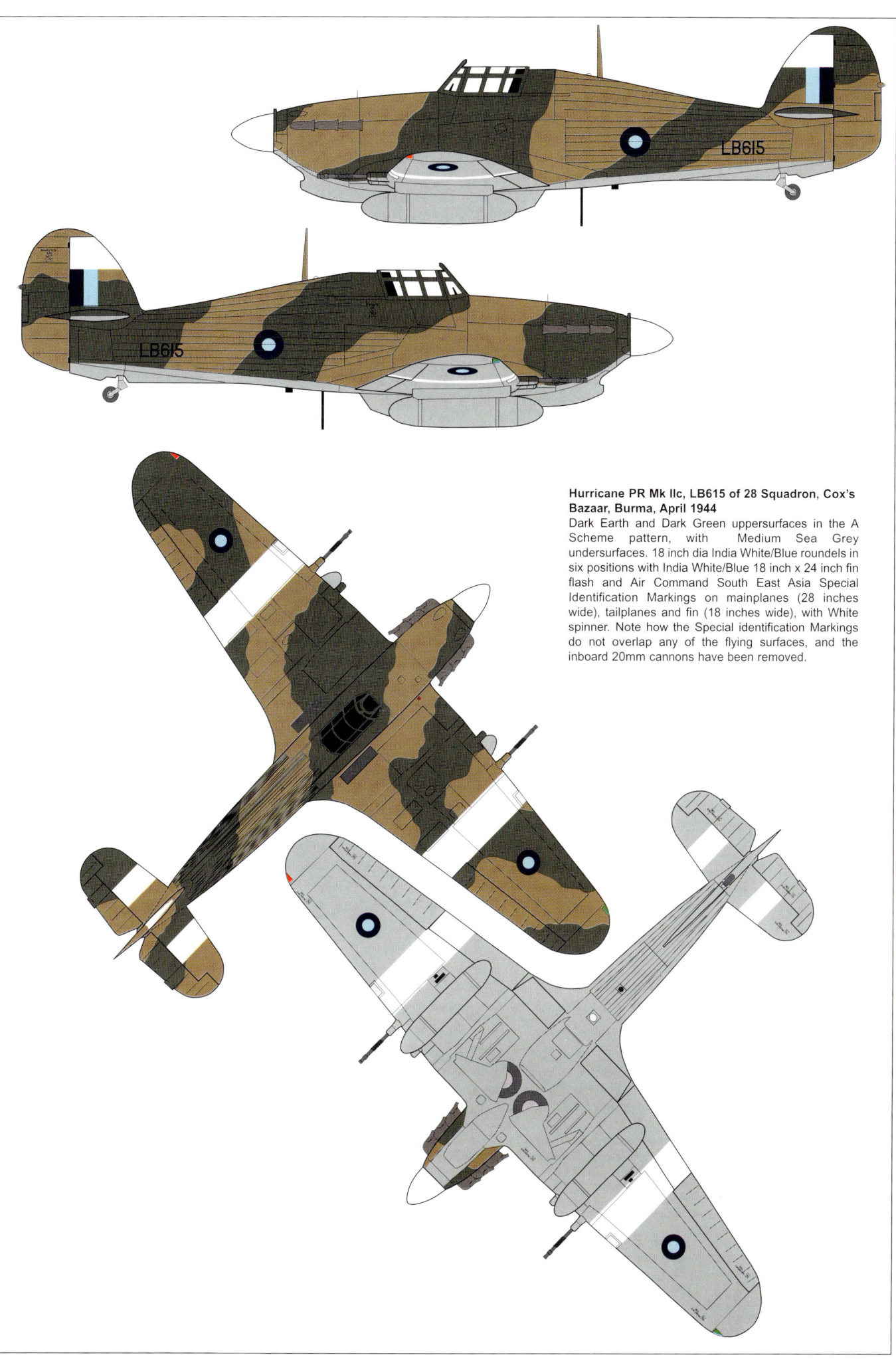

Hurricane PR Mk IIc, LB615 of 28 Squadron, Cox's Bazaar, Burma, April 1944

Dark Earth and Dark Green uppersurfaces in the A Scheme pattern, with Medium Sea Grey undersurfaces. 18 inch dia India White/Blue roundels in six positions with India White/Blue 18 inch x 24 inch fin flash and Air Command South East Asia Special Identification Markings on mainplanes (28 inches wide), tailplanes and fin (18 inches wide), with White spinner. Note how the Special identification Markings do not overlap any of the flying surfaces, and the inboard 20mm cannons have been removed.

Sea Hurricane Mk I, Z4936, KE•M of the Merchant Ship Fighter Unit, Speke, 1942
Extra Dark Sea Grey and Dark Slate Grey uppersurfaces, in the A Scheme pattern, with Sky undersurfaces. 49 inch Red/Blue National marking I upperwing roundels; 36 inch Red/White/Blue/Yellow National marking III fuselage roundels, and 32 inch Red/White/Blue National marking II underwing roundels. 24 inch x 24 inch Fin marking (i). Sky spinner and rear fuselage tail band. Approximately 30 inch high Sky codes. The original catapult cradle at the shore establishment was 3 feet higher than the version that was fitted aboard the CAM ships.

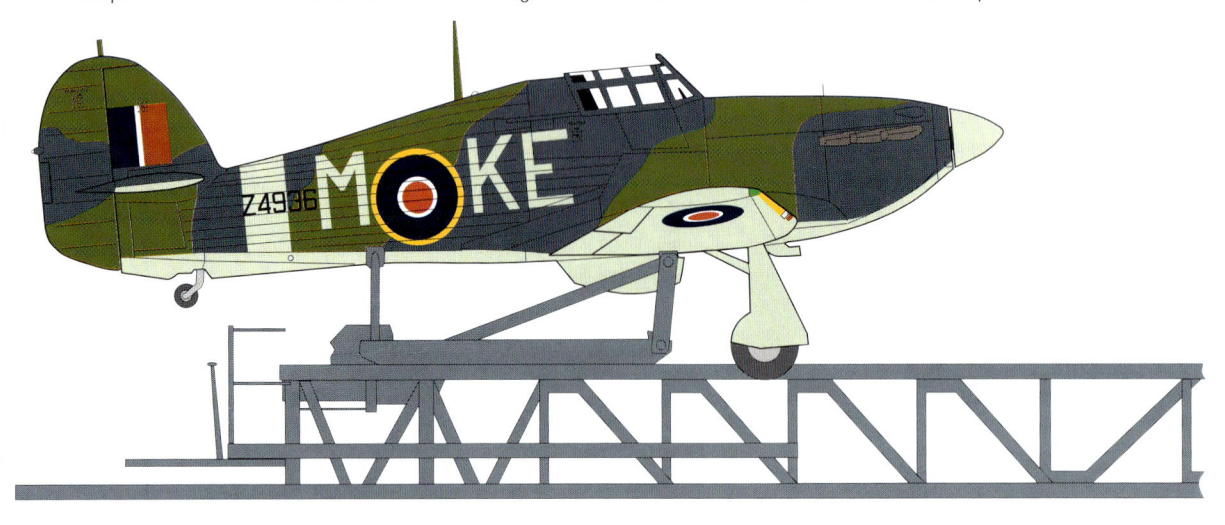

Sea Hurricane Mk I, V6756, NJ•L of the Merchant Ship Fighter Unit, aboard Catapult Aircraft Merchant (CAM) Ship *Empire Tide*, late 1941
Extra Dark Sea Grey and Dark Slate Grey uppersurfaces, in the A Scheme pattern, with Sky undersurfaces. 49 inch Red/Blue upperwing roundels; 35 inch Red/White/Blue/Yellow fuselage roundels, and approximately 50 inch Red/White/Blue underwing roundels. 24 inch x 27 inch fin flash. Sky spinner and rear fuselage tail band. Approximately 24 inch high Sky codes. The aircraft were loaded into the cradle at an angle of 5.25 degrees in order to maximise lift on launch.

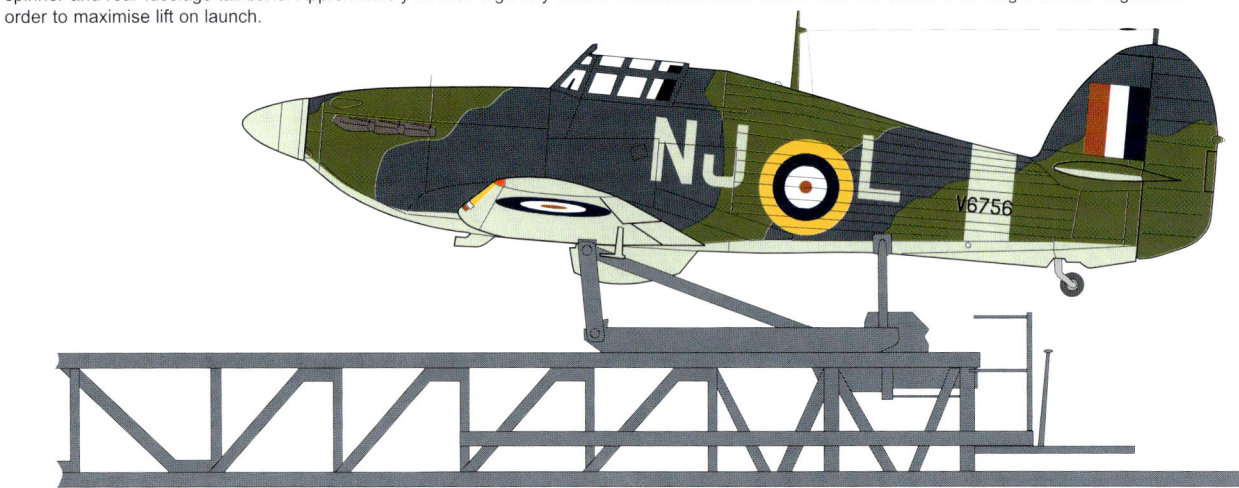

Sea Hurricane Mk I, Z4867, LU•Y of the Merchant Ship Fighter Unit, aboard an unknown Catapult Aircraft Merchant (CAM) Ship, late-1941
Extra Dark Sea Grey and Dark Slate Grey uppersurfaces, in the A Scheme pattern, with Sky undersurfaces. 49 inch Red/Blue upperwing roundels; 35 inch Red/White/Blue/Yellow fuselage roundels, and approximately 50 inch Red/White/Blue underwing roundels. 24 inch x 27 inch fin flash. Sky spinner and rear fuselage tail band. Approximately 24 inch high Sky codes. The catapult extended forwards by a further fifteen trusses.

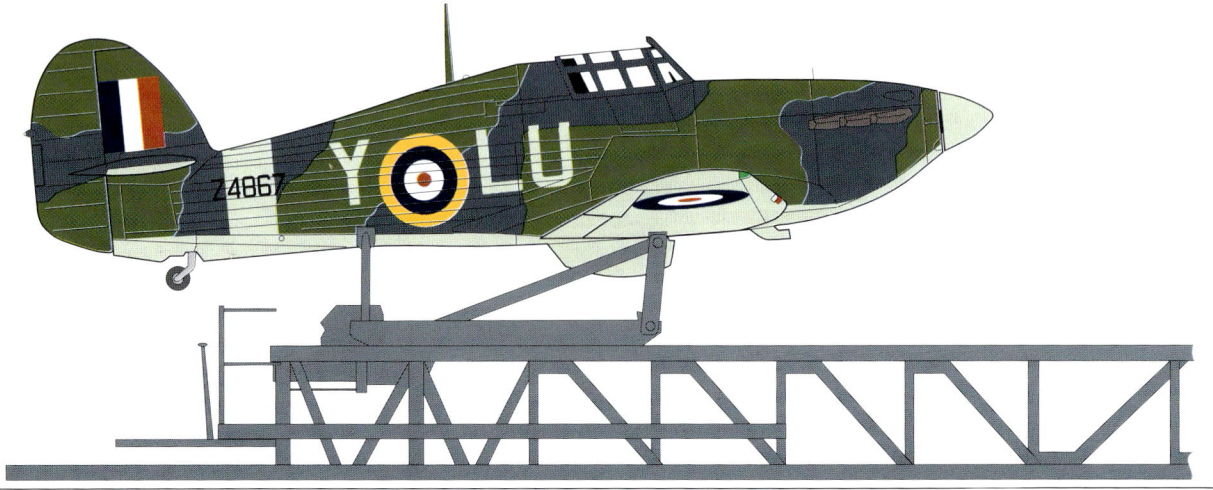

Sea Hurricane Mk I, W9219 of 880 Squadron, Fleet Air Arm, Arbroath, whilst working up, summer 1941
Extra Dark Sea Grey and Dark Slate Grey uppersurfaces, in the B Scheme pattern, with Sky Grey undersurfaces extending up the fuselage sides/fin and rudder in Pattern No 2. 49 inch Red/Blue upperwing roundels; 35 inch Red/White/Blue/Yellow fuselage roundels and approximately 50 inch Red/White/Blue underwing roundels. 24 inch x 27 inch fin flash. This scheme was very short-lived.

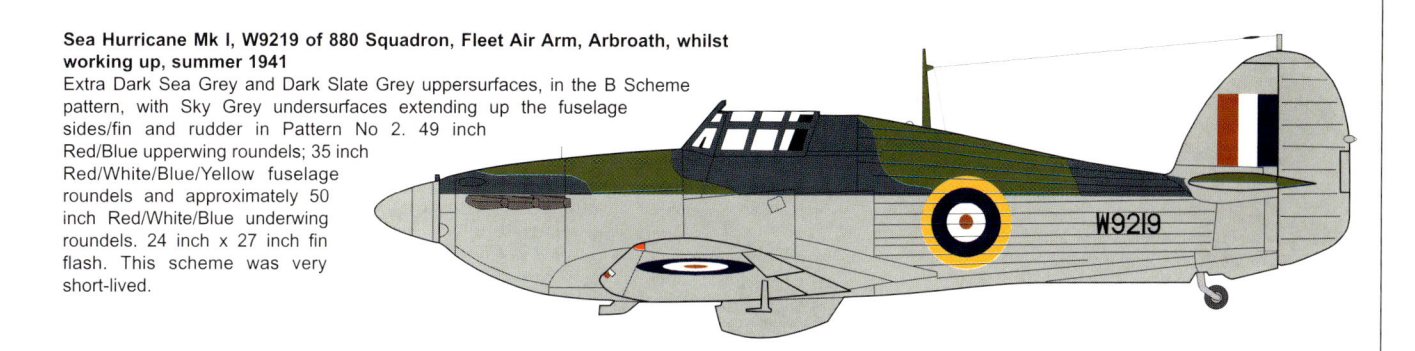

Sea Hurricane Mk Ib, Z4550, '6G' of 800 Squadron, Fleet Air Arm, *HMS Indomitable*, August 1942
Extra Dark Sea Grey and Dark Slate Grey uppersurfaces, in the B Scheme pattern, with Sky undersurfaces. 49 inch Red/Blue upperwing roundels; 35 inch Red/White/Blue/Yellow fuselage roundels and approximately 50 inch Red/White/Blue underwing roundels. 24 inch x 27 inch fin flash. Approximately 27 inch high individual aircraft letter on fuselage, with full code repeated on inboard leading edges of mainplanes in white, approx 12 inches high, (see inset). Night spinner. Note the white band around nose and lack of Sky rear fuselage tail band. Yellow wing leading edge stripes, outboard of the machine gun ports, applied for Operation Pedestal.

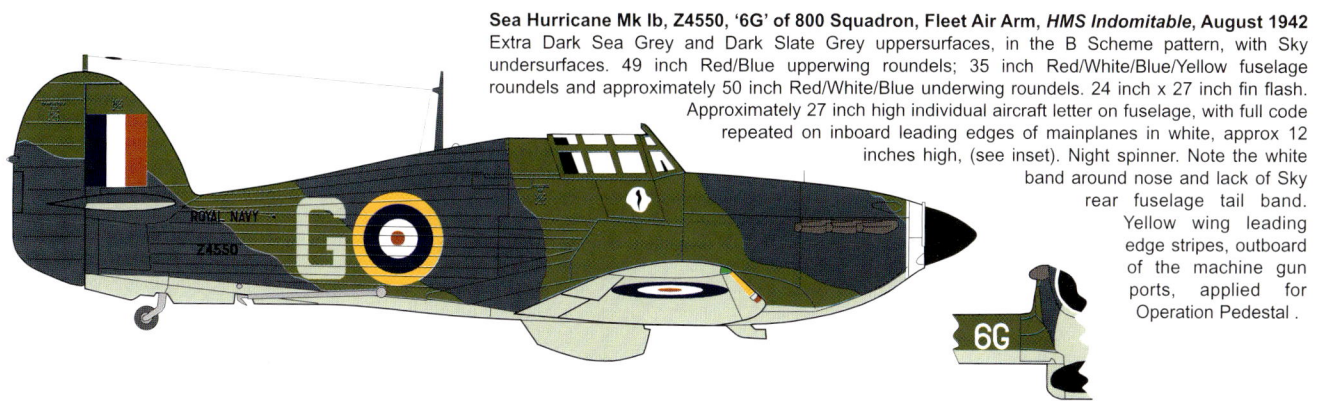

Sea Hurricane Mk Ib, P5206 '6C' of 800 Squadron, Fleet Air Arm, *HMS Indomitable*, August 1942
Extra Dark Sea Grey and Dark Slate Grey uppersurfaces, in the B Scheme pattern, with Sky undersurfaces. 49 inch Red/Blue upperwing roundels; 35 inch Red/White/Blue/Yellow fuselage roundels and approximately 50 inch Red/White/Blue underwing roundels. 24 inch x 27 inch fin flash. Approximately 27 inch high individual aircraft letter on fuselage, with full code repeated on inboard leading edges of mainplanes in white, approx 12 inches high, (see inset). Night spinner. Note the lack of Sky rear fuselage tail band. Yellow wing leading edges, outboard of machine gun ports, applied for Operation Pedestal.

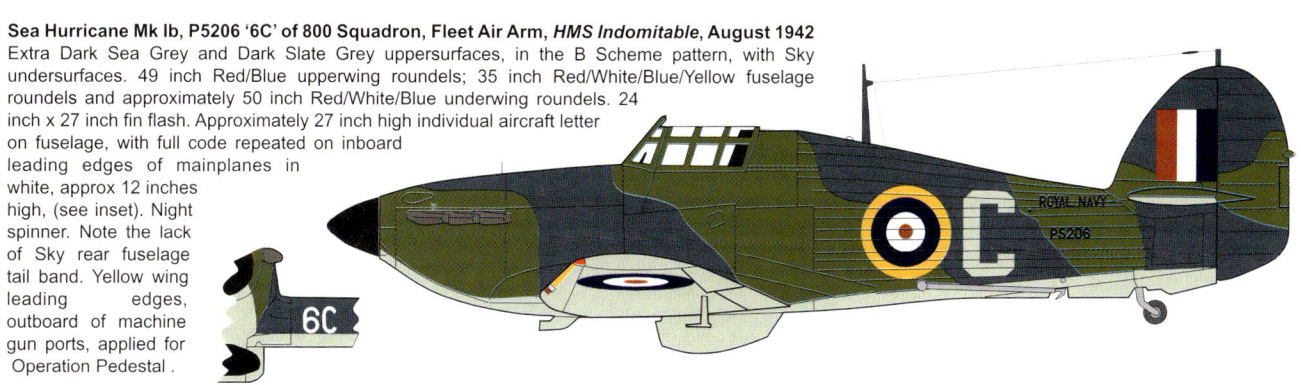

Sea Hurricane Mk Ib, AF955 '7E' of 880 Squadron, Fleet Air Arm, *HMS Indomitable*, August 1942
Extra Dark Sea Grey and Dark Slate Grey uppersurfaces, in the A Scheme pattern, with Sky undersurfaces. 49 inch Red/Blue upperwing roundels; 35 inch Red/White/Blue/Yellow fuselage roundels and approximately 50 inch Red/White/Blue underwing roundels. 24 inch x 27 inch fin flash. Approximately 27 inch high codes on fuselage. Sky spinner and rear fuselage tail band. Yellow wing leading edges, outboard of machine gun ports, applied for Operation Pedestal. Note the white band around nose with four rows of black checks.

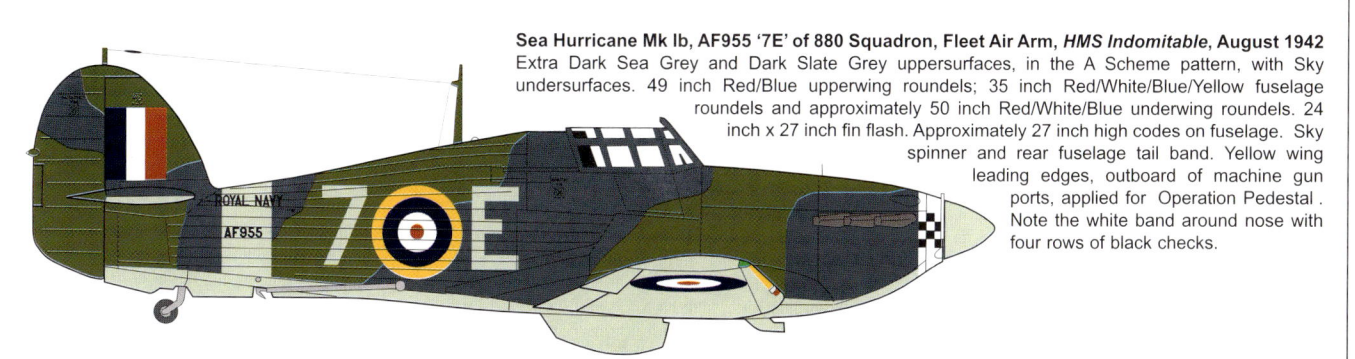

Sea Hurricane Mk Ib, AE966 '7F' of 880 Squadron, Fleet Air Arm, *HMS Indomitable*, August 1942
Extra Dark Sea Grey and Dark Slate Grey uppersurfaces, in the A Scheme pattern, with Sky undersurfaces. 49 inch Red/Blue upperwing roundels; 35 inch Red/White/Blue/Yellow fuselage roundels and approximately 50 inch Red/White/Blue underwing roundels. 24 inch x 27 inch fin flash. Approximately 27 inch high codes on fuselage. Sky spinner and rear fuselage tail band. Yellow wing leading edges, outboard of machine gun ports, applied for Operation Pedestal.

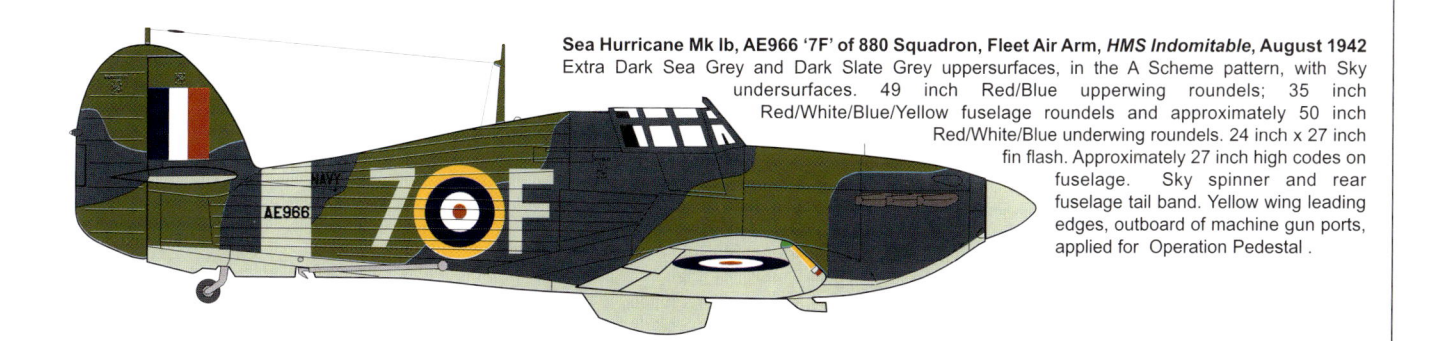

Sea Hurricane Mk Ib, Z7153 'F' of 801 Squadron, Fleet Air Arm, *HMS Eagle*, August 1942
Extra Dark Sea Grey and Dark Slate Grey uppersurfaces, in the A Scheme pattern, with Sky undersurfaces. 49 inch Red/Blue upperwing roundels; 35 inch Red/White/Blue/Yellow fuselage roundels and approximately 50 inch Red/White/Blue underwing roundels. 24 inch x 27 inch fin flash. Approximately 36 inch high individual aircraft letter on fuselage. Sky spinner but no rear fuselage tail band. Yellow wing leading edge stripes, (outboard of the landing lights), and Yellow fin applied for Operation Pedestal.

Sea Hurricane Mk Ib, V7077 'H' of 801 Squadron, Fleet Air Arm, *HMS Eagle*, August 1942
Extra Dark Sea Grey and Dark Slate Grey uppersurfaces, in the A Scheme pattern, with Sky undersurfaces. 49 inch Red/Blue (National marking I) upperwing roundels; 36 inch Red/White/Blue/Yellow (National marking III) fuselage roundels, and 32 inch Red/White/Blue (National marking II) underwing roundels. 24 inch x 24 inch Red/White/Blue (Fin marking (i)). Approximately 36 inch high individual aircraft letter on fuselage. Sky spinner but no rear fuselage tail band. Yellow wing leading edge stripes, (outboard of the landing lights), and Yellow fin applied for Operation Pedestal. This was one of four 801 Sqn Sea Hurricanes which survived the loss of *Eagle* during Operation Pedestal and was one of three aircraft which landed on *HMS Victorious* instead.

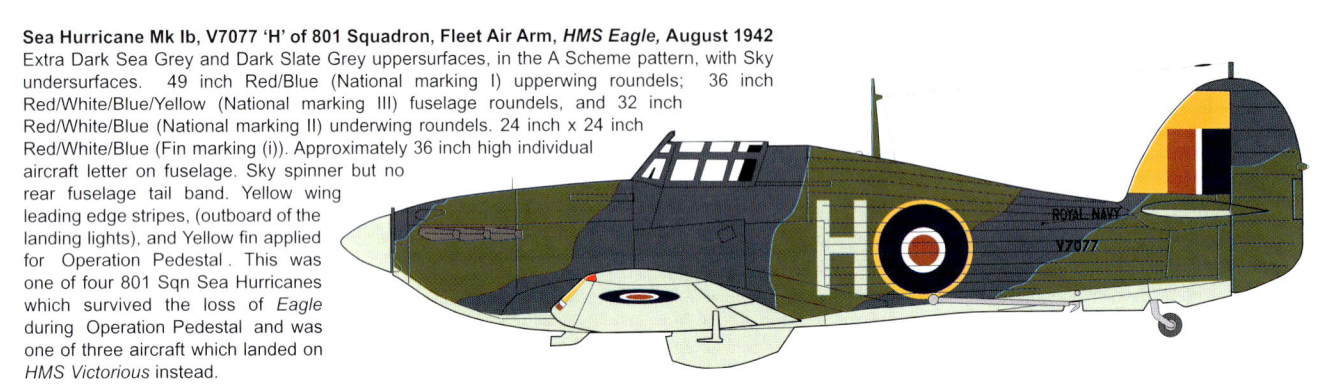

Sea Hurricane Mk Ib, V6695 'K' of 801 Squadron, Fleet Air Arm *HMS Eagle*, August 1942
Extra Dark Sea Grey and Dark Slate Grey uppersurfaces, in the B Scheme pattern, with Sky undersurfaces. 49 inch Red/Blue (National marking I) upperwing roundels; 36 inch Red/White/Blue/Yellow (National marking III) fuselage roundels, and 32 inch Red/White/Blue (National marking II) underwing roundels. 24 inch x 24 inch Red/White/Blue (Fin marking (i)). Approximately 36 inch high individual aircraft letter on fuselage. Sky spinner but no rear fuselage tail band. Yellow wing leading edge stripes, outboard of the landing lights - (see inset), and Yellow fin applied for Operation Pedestal. This was a late standard aircraft brought out from the UK for Pedestal

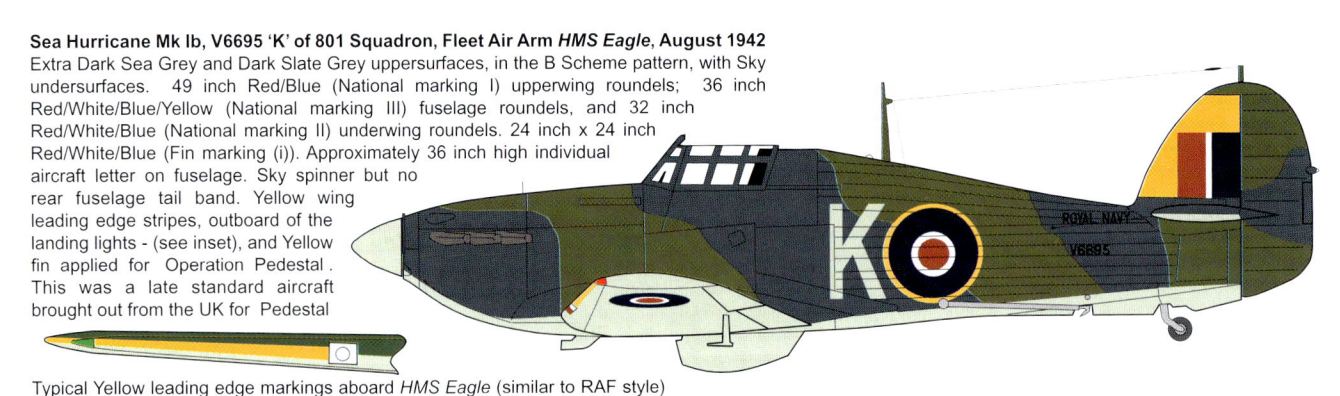

Typical Yellow leading edge markings aboard *HMS Eagle* (similar to RAF style)

Sea Hurricane Mk Ib, AF874 '7D' of 880 Squadron, Fleet Air Arm, *HMS Indomitable*, August 1942
Extra Dark Sea Grey and Dark Slate Grey uppersurfaces, in the B Scheme pattern, with Sky undersurfaces. 49 inch Red/Blue upperwing roundels; 35 inch Red/White/Blue/Yellow fuselage roundels and approximately 50 inch Red/White/Blue underwing roundels. 24 inch x 27 inch fin flash. Approximately 27 inch high codes on fuselage. Sky spinner and rear fuselage tail band. Yellow wing leading edges, outboard of machine gun ports, applied for Operation Pedestal. The code letters were painted parallel to the tapering fuselage stringers.

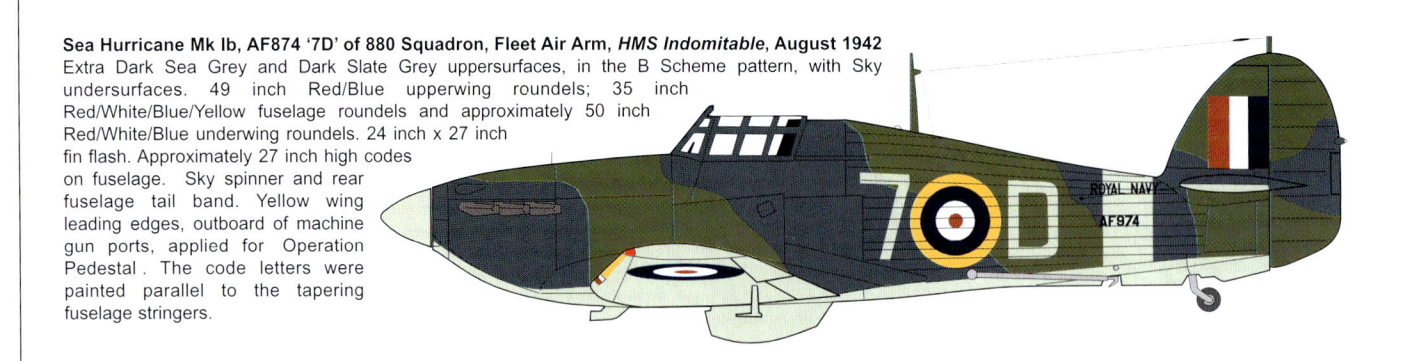

Sea Hurricane Mk Ib, Z4849 '7G' of 880 Squadron, Fleet Air Arm, *HMS Indomitable*, August 1942
Extra Dark Sea Grey and Dark Slate Grey uppersurfaces, in the A Scheme pattern, with Sky undersurfaces. 49 inch Red/Blue upperwing roundels; 35 inch Red/White/Blue/Yellow fuselage roundels and approximately 50 inch Red/White/Blue underwing roundels. 24 inch x 27 inch fin flash. Approximately 27 inch high codes on fuselage. Sky spinner and rear fuselage tail band. Yellow wing leading edges, outboard of machine gun ports, applied for Operation Pedestal. This particular aircraft, flown by Sub/Lt Hugh Popham, crash-landed aboard *HMS Victorious* during Operation Pedestal.

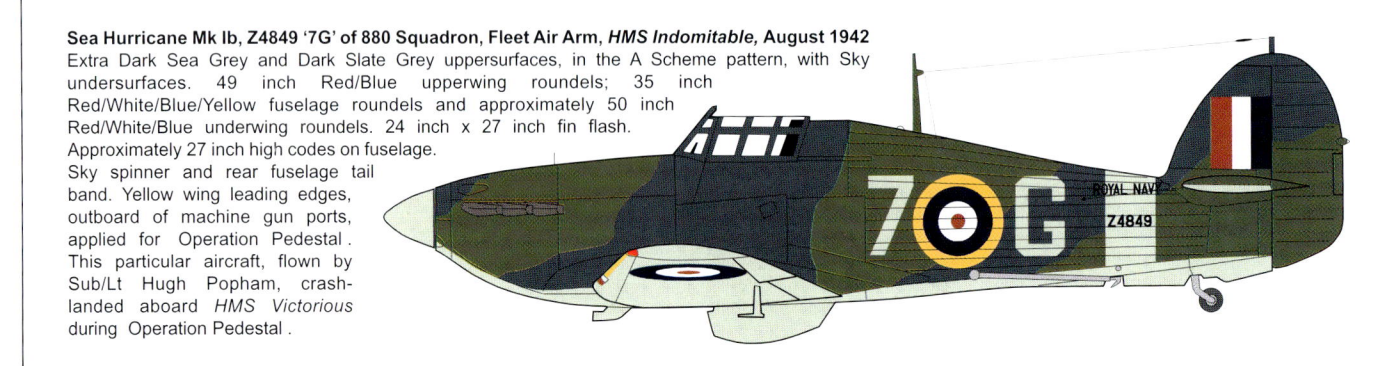

Sea Hurricane Mk Ib, W9134 '7Y' of 885 Squadron, *HMS Victorious*, August 1942
Extra Dark Sea Grey and Dark Slate Grey uppersurfaces, in the A Scheme pattern, with Sky undersurfaces. 49 inch Red/Blue upperwing roundels; 35 inch Red/White/Blue/Yellow fuselage roundels and approximately 50 inch Red/White/Blue underwing roundels. 24 inch x 27 inch fin flash. This was the only aircraft aboard *Victorious* to still carry the older style National markings. Approximately 24 inch high codes on fuselage, in Red, in *Victorious* distinctive aft position. Sky spinner and rear fuselage tail band. Yellow wing leading edge stripes, (outboard of the machine gun ports), applied for Operation Pedestal

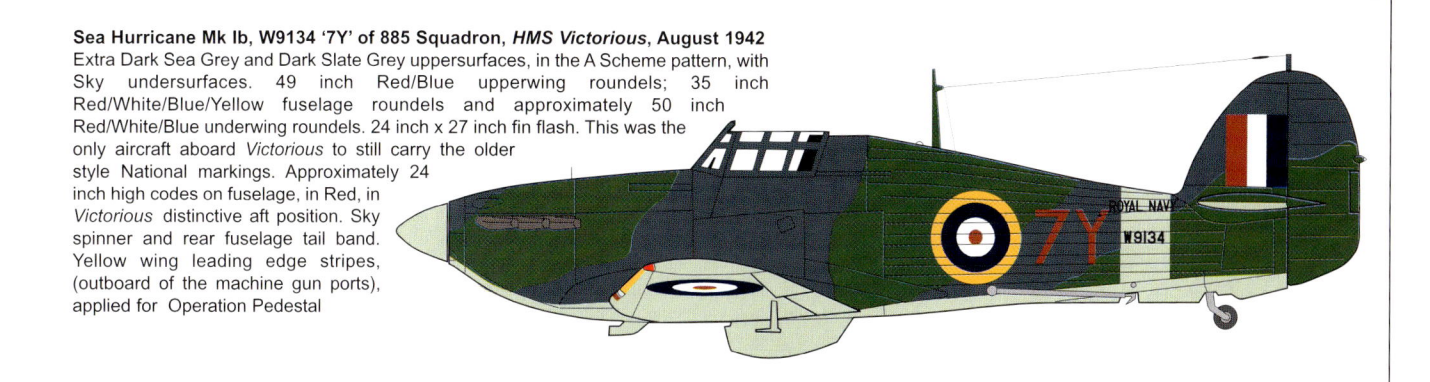

Sea Hurricane Mk Ib, V7506 '7T' of 885 Squadron, Fleet Air Arm, *HMS Victorious*, August 1942
Extra Dark Sea Grey and Dark Slate Grey uppersurfaces, in the B Scheme pattern, with Sky undersurfaces. 49 inch Red/Blue (National marking I) upperwing roundels; 36 inch Red/White/Blue/Yellow (National marking III) fuselage roundels, and 32 inch Red/White/Blue (National marking II) underwing roundels. 24 inch x 24 inch Red/White/Blue (Fin marking (i)). Approximately 24 inch high codes on fuselage in Sky. Sky spinner and rear fuselage tail band. Yellow wing leading edge stripes, (outboard of the landing lights), and Yellow fin applied for Operation Pedestal .

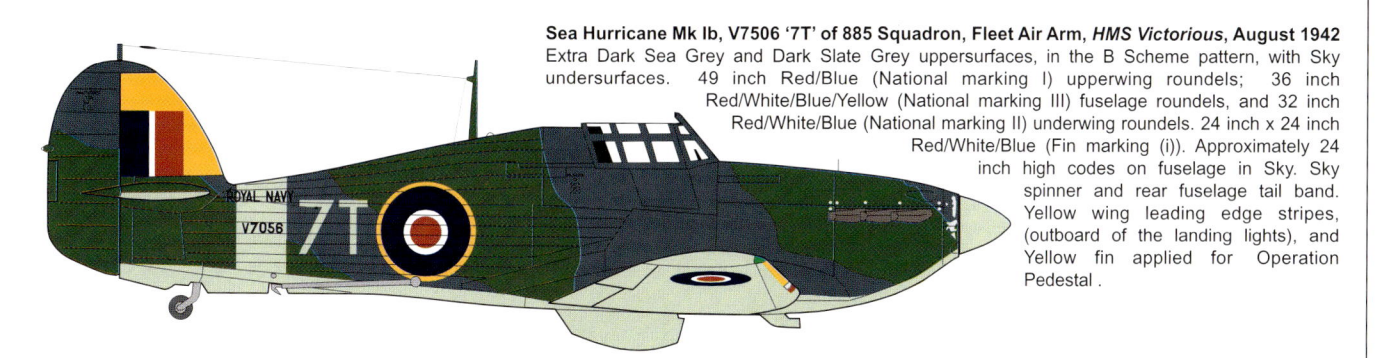

Sea Hurricane Mk Ib, (serial unknown) '7U' of 885 Squadron, Fleet Air Arm, *HMS Victorious*, August 1942
Extra Dark Sea Grey and Dark Slate Grey uppersurfaces, in the B Scheme pattern, with Sky undersurfaces. 49 inch Red/Blue (National marking I) upperwing roundels; 36 inch Red/White/Blue/Yellow (National marking III) fuselage roundels, and 32 inch Red/White/Blue (National marking II) underwing roundels. 24 inch x 24 inch Red/White/Blue (Fin marking (i)). Approximately 24 inch high codes on fuselage in Sky. Sky spinner and rear fuselage tail band. Yellow wing leading edge stripes, (outboard of the landing lights), and Yellow fin applied for Operation Pedestal .

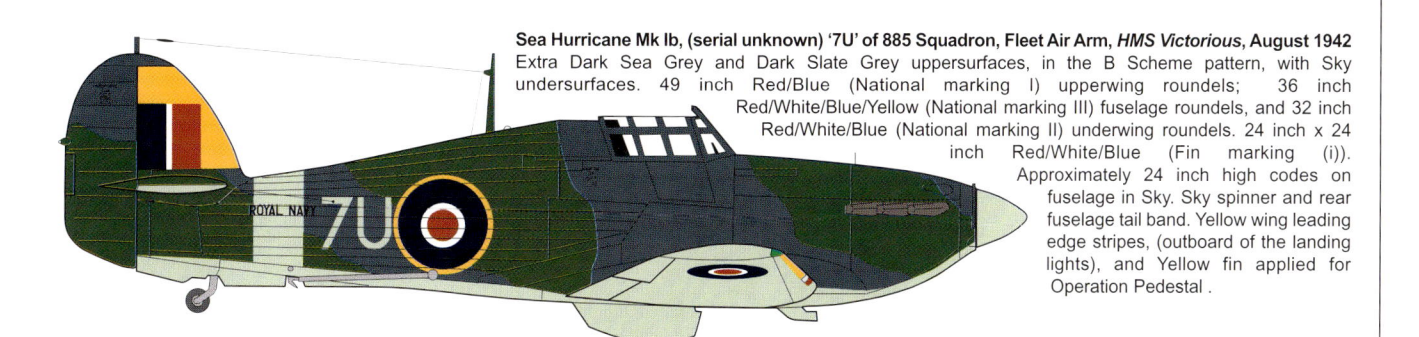

Hurricane Mk I, Z4227 of the Royal Navy Fighter Squadron, Western Desert, August 1942
Dark Earth and Middle Stone uppersurfaces, in the A Scheme pattern, with Sky Blue undersurfaces. 49 inch Red/Blue upperwing roundels; 35 inch Red/White/Blue/Yellow fuselage roundels, and 50 inch Red/White/Blue underwing roundels. 24 inch x 27 inch fin flash. Night spinner. This unit was a temporary amalgamation of 803, 805 and 806 Squadrons, for operations in the Western Desert. 803 and 806 Squadrons had disembarked from *HMS Formidable* following battle damage and 805 Squadron was temporarily shore-based. The aircraft used were borrowed from the RAF.

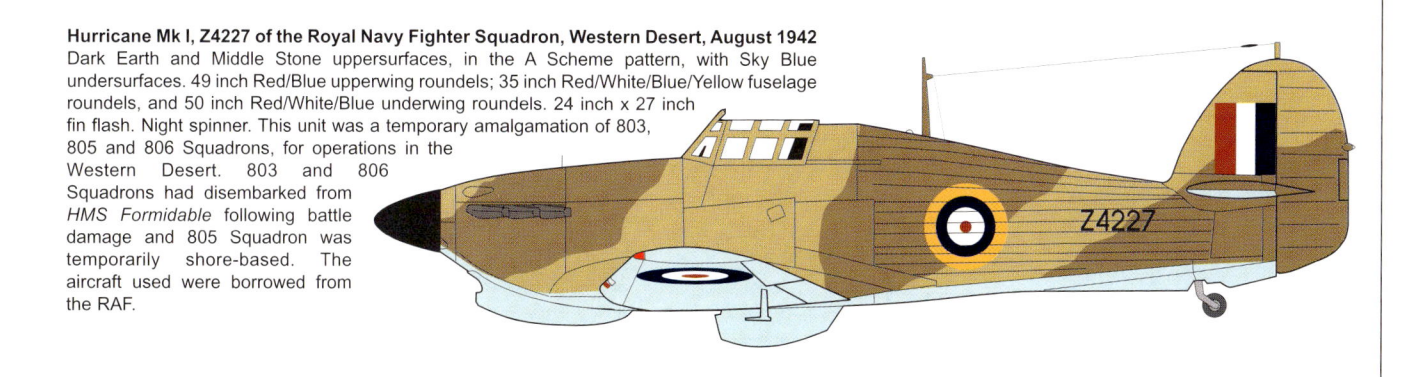

Sea Hurricane Mk X, AM277 of 891 Squadron, FAA, *HMS Dasher*, November 1942
Extra Dark Sea Grey and Dark Slate Grey uppersurfaces, in the A Scheme pattern, with Sky undersurfaces. 49 inch Red/Blue (National marking I) upperwing roundels thinly outlined in Yellow; 36 inch Red/White/Blue/Yellow (National marking III) fuselage roundels, and 32 inch Red/White/Blue (National marking II) underwing roundels - all overpainted with white US-style stars. The 24 inch x 24 inch Red/White/Blue (Fin marking (i)) was painted out. Dark Slate Grey spinner.
This aircraft crash-landed at St Leu, Algeria, on 8 November 1942 following combat with French fighters during Operation Torch , the Allied landings in North Africa, (see also the four-view of JS327 on page 46).

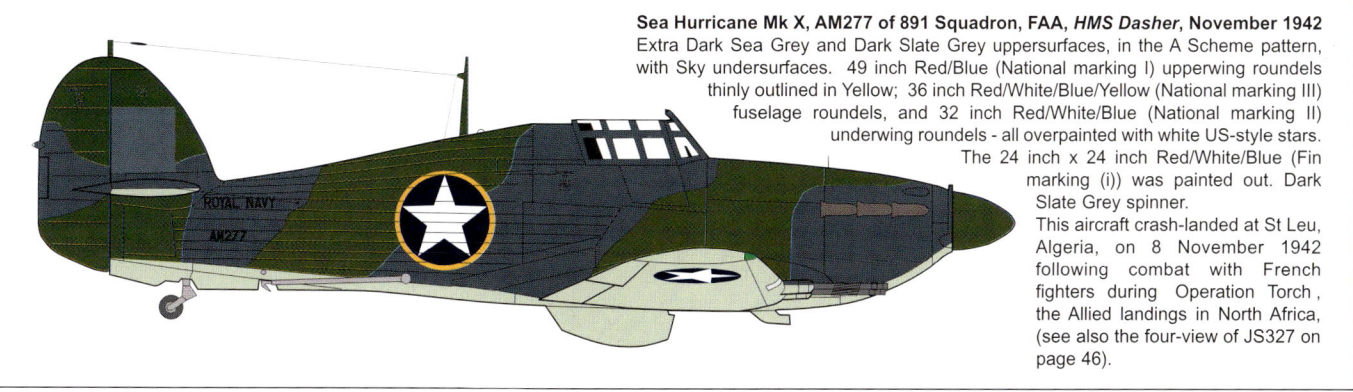

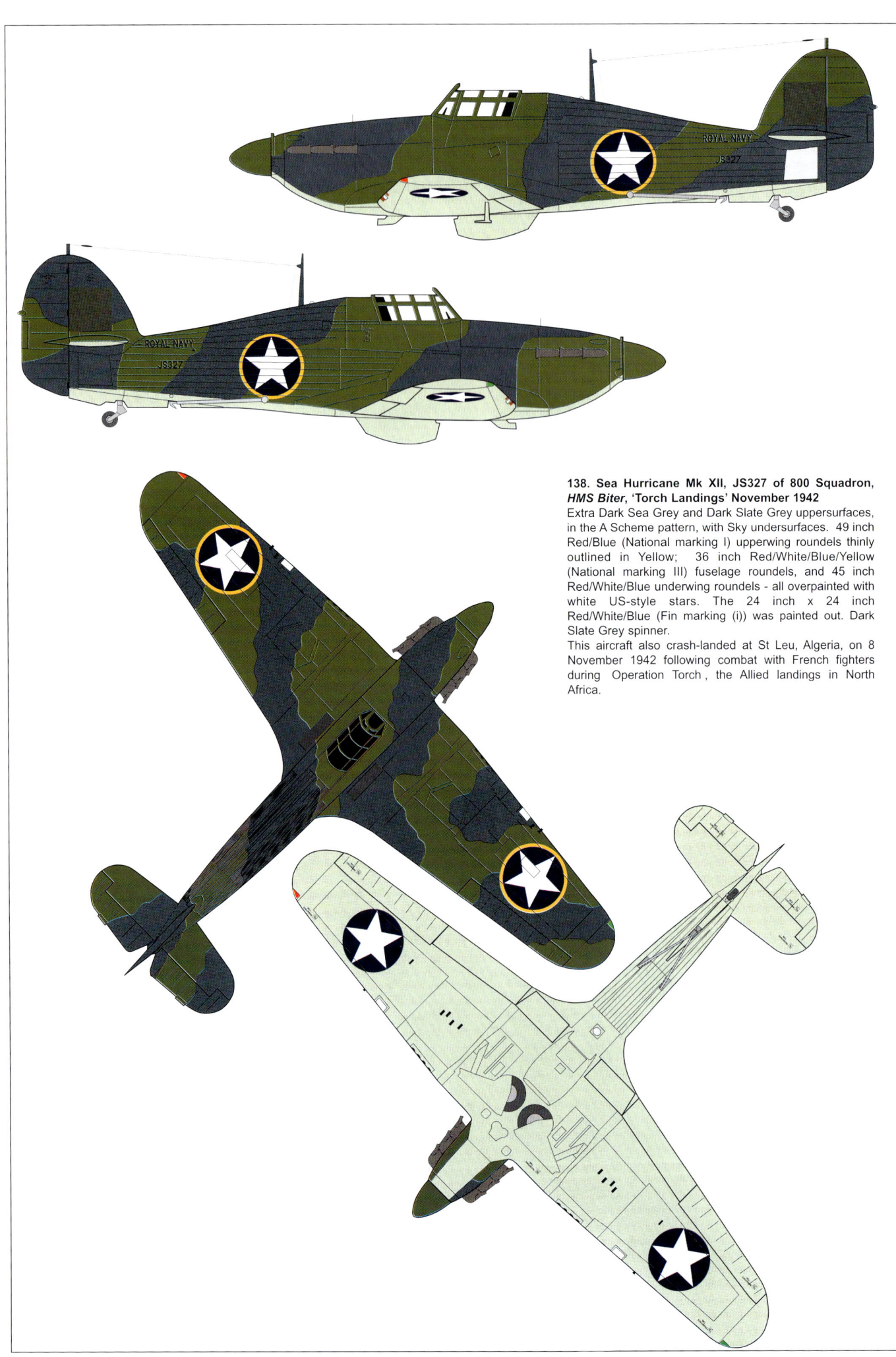

138. Sea Hurricane Mk XII, JS327 of 800 Squadron, *HMS Biter*, 'Torch Landings' November 1942

Extra Dark Sea Grey and Dark Slate Grey uppersurfaces, in the A Scheme pattern, with Sky undersurfaces. 49 inch Red/Blue (National marking I) upperwing roundels thinly outlined in Yellow; 36 inch Red/White/Blue/Yellow (National marking III) fuselage roundels, and 45 inch Red/White/Blue underwing roundels - all overpainted with white US-style stars. The 24 inch x 24 inch Red/White/Blue (Fin marking (i)) was painted out. Dark Slate Grey spinner.

This aircraft also crash-landed at St Leu, Algeria, on 8 November 1942 following combat with French fighters during Operation Torch, the Allied landings in North Africa.

Sea Hurricane Mk I, V7438, Y1•C of 759 Squadron, Fleet Air Arm, Yeovilton, August 1942
Extra Dark Sea Grey and Dark Slate Grey uppersurfaces, in the A Scheme pattern, with Sky undersurfaces. 49 inch Red/Blue (National marking I) upperwing roundels; 36 inch Red/White/Blue/Yellow (National marking III) fuselage roundels, and 32 inch Red/White/Blue (National marking II) underwing roundels. 24 inch x 24 inch Red/White/Blue (Fin marking (i)). Approximately 30 inch high codes on fuselage in Yellow. Sky spinner. This unit served as the Fleet Fighter School Squadron.

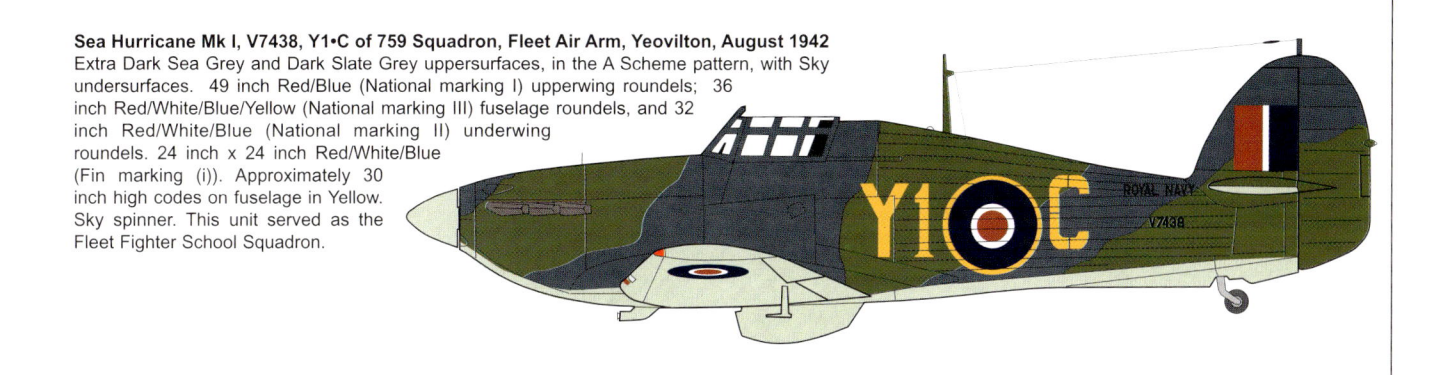

Sea Hurricane Mk Ib, Z4039 of 760 Squadron, Fleet Air Arm, Yeovilton, August 1942
Extra Dark Sea Grey and Dark Slate Grey uppersurfaces, in the A Scheme pattern, with Sky undersurfaces. 49 inch Red/Blue (National marking I) upperwing roundels; 36 inch Red/White/Blue/Yellow (National marking III) fuselage roundels, and 32 inch Red/White/Blue (National marking II) underwing roundels. 24 inch x 24 inch Red/White/Blue (Fin marking (i)). Red spinner. This unit served as the Fleet Fighter Pool Squadron.

Sea Hurricane Mk Ia, Z4822, W9•D of 760 Squadron, Fleet Air Arm, Yeovilton, August 1942
Extra Dark Sea Grey and Dark Slate Grey uppersurfaces, in the B Scheme pattern, with Sky undersurfaces. 49 inch Red/Blue (National marking I) upperwing roundels; 36 inch Red/White/Blue/Yellow (National marking III) fuselage roundels, and 32 inch Red/White/Blue (National marking II) underwing roundels. 24 inch x 24 inch Red/White/Blue (Fin marking (i)). Night spinner. Approximately 24 inch high Red codes. This aircraft's paint finish was extremely worn and weathered with large areas of previous camouflage scheme(s) showing through.

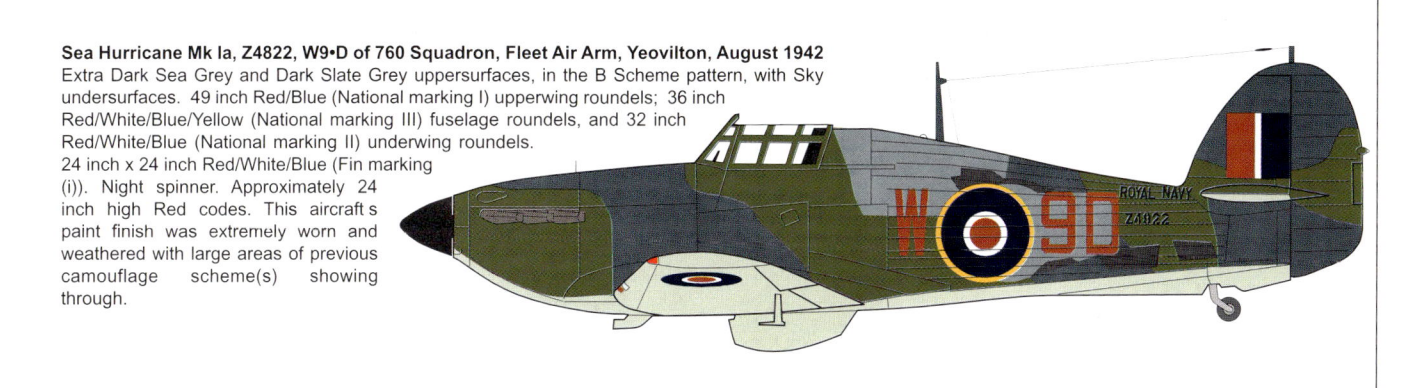

Sea Hurricane Mk IIb, (serial unknown), M2•K of 768 Squadron, Fleet Air Arm, Macrihanish, August 1943
Extra Dark Sea Grey and Dark Slate Grey uppersurfaces, in the A Scheme pattern, with Sky undersurfaces. 49 inch Red/Blue (National marking I) upperwing roundels; 36 inch Red/White/Blue/Yellow (National marking III) fuselage roundels, and 32 inch Red/White/Blue (National marking II) underwing roundels. 24 inch x 24 inch Red/White/Blue (Fin marking (i)). Red spinner. Approximately 24 inch high Yellow codes. This unit was a Deck Landing Training Squadron, operating with the Light Carrier *HMS Argus*.

Sea Hurricane Mk IIc, NF728, K1•F of 768 Squadron, Fleet Air Arm, Inskip, December 1944
Extra Dark Sea Grey and Dark Slate Grey uppersurfaces, in the A Scheme pattern, with Sky undersurfaces. 49 inch Red/Blue (National marking I) upperwing roundels; 36 inch Red/White/Blue/Yellow (National marking III) fuselage roundels, and 32 inch Red/White/Blue (National marking II) underwing roundels. 24 inch x 24 inch Red/White/Blue (Fin marking (i)). Sky spinner. Approximately 30 inch high Red codes. This aircraft was fitted with 60lb Rocket Projectiles.

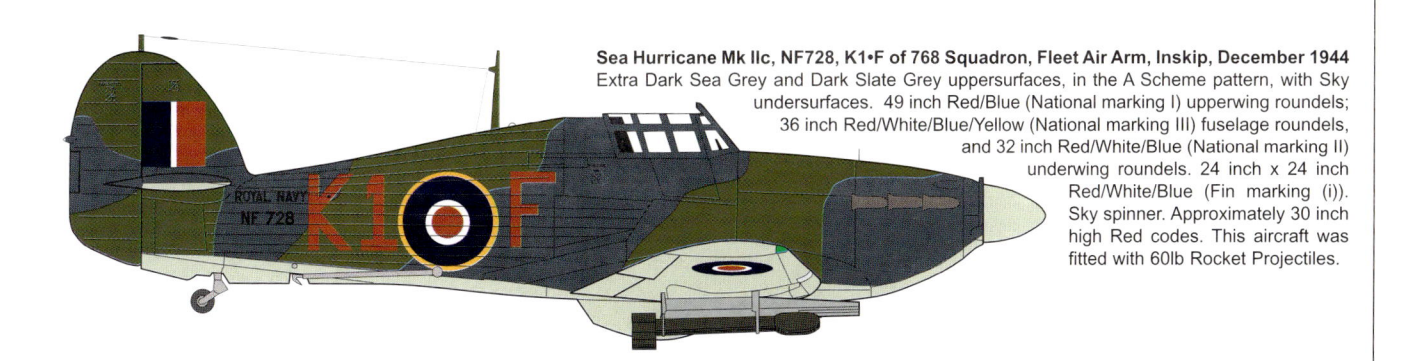

HURRICANE CAMOUFLAGE AND MARKINGS IN THE MIDDLE EASTERN THEATRE OF OPERATIONS

Until June 1940, much of the British Empire had not been directly affected by the hostilities with Germany but all that changed when Italy entered the War on 10 June. At that time there was not a single RAF squadron anywhere in the Mediterranean or Middle East equipped with 'modern' fighters. It was therefore essential to send reinforcements to the Mediterranean to protect the Suez Canal and Malta, and the only modern fighter of which Britain possessed suitably adequate stocks was the Hurricane.

The first Hurricane to reach the Middle East had been L1699, which was despatched to Khartoum for tropical trials just prior to the outbreak of war, so when the hostilities eventually spread to the Mediterranean, the Hurricane was known to be suitable for operations in the region. On 17 June 1940, six Hurricanes equipped with the long range tanks, developed for the abortive Norwegian campaign, were despatched to Egypt via the South of France. In the event, only four Hurricanes got as far as Malta where they were retained as part of the island's defence force.

When France surrendered, this route was no longer available to fly Hurricanes to the Middle East and an alternative route had to be found. Despatch of further Hurricanes to Malta was undertaken by the simple expedient of flying twelve aircraft of 418 Flight off the aircraft carrier *HMS Argus* on 2 August 1940.

Photographs of these aircraft which were taken on board *Argus* and later on Malta, suggest that they were some of, if not the first, aircraft to be finished in Dark Earth and Middle Stone on the uppersurfaces with either Sky, (or one of the Sky 'substitute colours' being used at this time), on the undersurfaces.

At this time, Middle Stone was a new colour in the RAF's camouflage palette. Unlike all the other camouflage colours then in use on aircraft, with the exception of the Sky 'substitutes', Middle Stone had not been invented by the RAE. Instead, like the Sky 'substitute colours', it appears to have been chosen directly from BS 381 (1930) where it was included as colour No 62.

At the time of writing, we can only speculate as to why this colour was chosen when there were several other colours which had been selected for overland use in tropical areas through trials before the war. Like the Sky 'substitute colours', it might have simply been the case that Middle Stone was available when the other colours were not!

These Hurricanes, along with the four which were already on the island, were given the title of 261 Squadron. 261 Sqn does not appear to have been allocated any squadron codes as photographs of these Hurricanes on Malta show only the individual aircraft letter being carried, possibly in White. With a squadron now established on the island, Malta appeared to be capable of looking after itself for the time being, and some thought could be given as to how Hurricanes could be supplied to Egypt.

After considering the problem, it was decided to fly them there overland by employing the landing grounds established by Imperial Airways in the 1930s. These stretched from the Gold Coast on the West coast of Africa to Egypt, and ultimately this route came to be known by the name of the base on the West African coast where it originated as the Takoradi Route. The Hurricanes were accompanied by a Blenheim to navigate on behalf of the whole formation and the first such flight took place during September 1940.

As this route took the Hurricanes over vast uninhabited spaces, the rear of the fuselage spine and upper surfaces of the tailplanes were painted White using an easily removable distemper in order to assist search parties in locating the aircraft should it be forced to land for any reason. By this means the numbers of Hurricanes in Egypt could be slowly built up and by the beginning of 1941, Egypt had two operational Hurricane Squadrons, Nos 274 and 73.

A replacement for Sky

The camouflage and markings applied to Hurricanes in the Middle East in early 1941 are still open to question to some extent. Whilst it is known that they were supposed to be camouflaged on their uppersurfaces in Dark Earth and Middle Stone, with Middle Stone being used in place of Dark Green, it is not known how widely this was actually carried out. A further question exists over the colour applied to the undersurfaces. Whilst in the UK, Sky had become well established in RAF service by December 1940, the extent to which this colour was applied to

Heading: Tropicalised Hurricane Mk I, Z4641, possibly of 237 (Rhodesian) Sqn., circa mid-1942. Camouflage scheme appears to be Dark Earth and Middle Stone uppersurfaces with Sky Blue undersides with pre-May 1942 markings.

Left: Hurricane Mk I, P3731 'J' of 261 Sqn., at Ta' Qali, Malta. Twelve Hurricanes were taken to Malta by *HMS Argus* in August 1940 and were amongst the first aircraft to be finished in the Dark Earth and Middle Stone scheme, probably with Sky Blue undersides.

Right: Tropicalised Hurricane Mk Is jointly operated by Nos 80 and 274 Squadrons in the summer of 1940. P2544 YK·T in the foreground is still in the Temperate Land Scheme of Dark Earth and Dark Green uppersurfaces, but with Sky Blue undersides.

Below: A Middle Stone/Dark Earth/Sky Blue finished Hurricane Mk I, (probably of No 3 Sqn RAAF, based at Benina in 1941), with its nose and wing leading edges overpainted in Italian style camouflage.

RAF aircraft sent to the Middle East is not so well known.

When the first Blenheims to be finished with 'Sky' undersurfaces had been flown out to the Middle East in the early part of 1940, Middle East Command had rejected Sky as a camouflage colour because it was considered to be "too light and too green" for the region. As a consequence Middle East Command mixed its own colour which was a blue of some sort and petitioned the Air Ministry in London to match the colour and then ensure that it was applied to all day flying aircraft sent to the Middle East.

By the end of December 1940, the RAE had produced a new blue colour for use in the Middle East and named it Azure Blue. Unfortunately, it is not known with any degree of certainty when this colour started to appear on the production line or become available from stores to the squadrons in the Middle East. Nor is it known whether any other colour was applied to Hurricanes despatched to the Middle East in the meantime in place of Sky. Photographs consistently show a light tone which might be suggestive of Sky Blue, as it is assumed that Sky was not an option. Camouflage schemes aside, apart from the absence of the Sky spinner and rear fuselage band markings, the Hurricanes in the Middle East were otherwise marked in the same way as those in the UK including the temporary black underside to the port wing.

PR Blues

Some Hurricanes were converted into photographic reconnaissance aircraft by the Service Depot at Heliopolis, which

Right: Hurricane Mk I, P2627 of an unidentified unit, in what appears to be Night/White mainplane undersurfaces, but what is more likely to be a Special Night port underwing on Sky or Sky Blue undersurfaces. Uppersurfaces are Dark Earth and Dark Green.

eventually went on to serve with No 2 PRU. The first three Hurricanes to be modified, (designated PR Mk I), flew in January 1941, followed by another five in March. It is not known for certain exactly what colour these very early PR Hurricane conversions were painted in, although it has been suggested that it might have been either Light or Dark Mediterranean Blue. However, it is known that the majority of PR Hurricane conversions were camouflaged in a very dark blue colour which was even darker than the Blue used in the National markings.

This colour is said to have been mixed from 5 gallons of an ICI colour called 'Bosun Blue' to which was added 3lb of Black pigment and 16lb of Zinc powder and turpentine. The resulting colour has been described as 'Royal blue' which was fractionally darker than FS 35109. The same colour is thought to have been applied to the Hurricane PR Mk IIs converted during late 1942 to early 1943, many of which subsequently went to No 3 PRU in India.

Sand and Spinach

Possibly one of the most contentious colour schemes applied to Hurricanes anywhere was that which has been colloquially called the 'sand and spinach' scheme. This involved the repainting the front of the engine cowling and the leading edges of the mainplanes in a scheme which was similar in both colour and pattern to that used by the *Regia Aeronautica* (Italian Air Force). Exactly what colours were used is unknown, but it is quite possible that Italian paints were used as significant gains were made from the Italians during Wavell's offensive which opened on 8 December 1940, and lasted through to February 1941. It is quite possible that Italian aircraft paints were amongst the materiel which fell into British hands.

The reasons why this scheme was adopted appear to have been lost in the mists of time, but may be associated with the idea that the Hurricane squadrons wished to appear as Italian aircraft when seen from head-on by ground forces whilst either engaged on reconnaissance or ground attack missions. At the time this scheme is believed to have been used, circa February/March 1941, the Italians were successfully counter-attacking along the North African coast and driving British forces back towards Egypt. Under these circumstances, even a few moments of uncertainty that such camouflage might provide would be a positive asset for the Hurricanes.

Night underwing

As has already been mentioned, the black identification marking had been reintroduced to the under surface of the port wing in the UK in December 1940, and this also appears to have been used on some, if not all, Hurricanes in the Middle East. It is possible that the black port wing marking may have remained in use in the Middle East for slightly longer than it did in the UK. In Britain, the

Above: Hurricane Mk I, Z4189 'L' flew from Malta in the summer of 1941 in what is believed to have been the Dark Green and Middle Stone scheme with Sky Blue undersurfaces. The aircraft later served with No 73 Sqn in the Western desert.

Right: Hurricane Mk IIb, BD776 WG·F of 128 Sqn., based in West Africa circa late 1942, in Ocean Grey/Dark Green uppersurfaces with Medium Sea Grey undersides. Note the unit's distinctive Red/White/Blue spinner.

marking was dropped in April 1941, but photographs show this marking still in use during the fighting over Crete during May 1941.

By August 1941, the camouflage of aircraft in Overseas Theatres appears to have undergone something of a rethink. During that month an AMO was issued stating that the camouflage of operational aircraft for service abroad was to consist of either Dark Green and Dark Earth which was the Temperate Land Scheme, or Dark Green and 'Midstone' which was now named as the Tropical Land Scheme. Interestingly this AMO makes no mention of Azure Blue, citing Sky instead. Thus the camouflage applied to Hurricanes in the Middle East in 1941 is open to question and such photographs as exist are open to interpretation.

Malta Hurricanes

With the establishment of Hurricane squadrons on Malta, the island did prove capable of looking after itself to a large extent and further Hurricane deliveries were made during 1941 in the face of the worst the enemy could do. During this period the camouflage schemes carried by the Hurricanes no doubt reflected the changing policy leading to a mix of Dark Green/Dark Earth; Dark Green/Middle Stone; and Dark Earth/Middle Stone on the upper surfaces with a light colour such as Sky Blue or Sky on the under surfaces. As with the Hurricanes in North Africa, it is not currently known when Azure Blue was introduced. A variety of colours were also apparent in the application of squadron codes with Medium Sea Grey being used by 242 Sqn, White by 605 Sqn and Yellow by 249 Sqn.

At the end of August 1941, the Malta Night Fighter Unit was formed with twelve Hurricanes at Ta Qali to combat the nuisance raids that were being sent over the island throughout the night. In the absence of Radar, the aircraft were guided solely by searchlights and managed to obtain such good results that the number of raids decreased.

Like the Night Fighters in the UK these Hurricanes were finished in Special Night overall, but unlike the Night Fighters in the UK, their markings were modified slightly. The usual fuselage roundel was modified into a Red and Blue roundel and no codes appear to have been carried. The fuselage serial appears to have been applied in Medium Sea Grey although the fin flash appears to be unchanged. Following the success of this unit, it was formally recognised in December 1941 as 1435 Flight.

By the second half of 1941 the Hurricanes operating over Malta by day found themselves outclassed as fighters by the advent of the Messerschmitt Bf 109F, and in March 1942 Spitfires began to arrive on the island to take up the load. However, Hurricanes continued to play a part in the island's defence well in to the summer of 1942.

West Africa

Although found to be outclassed by the latest types of German and Italian fighters, the Hurricane was thought to still be capable of holding its own against the types operated by the Vichy French in West Africa. 128 Squadron was formed at Sierra Leone in October 1941 flying Hurricanes to counter the threat posed by Vichy French aircraft to British maritime activity along the West African coast. The Hurricanes of this squadron marked their spinners in a very distinctive way using Red, White and Blue rings, with the Red on the extreme tip of the spinner. The squadron was disbanded in March 1943 after the invasion of French North Africa had resulted in the *Armée de l'Air* (French Air Force) in the region joining the Allies.

National markings changes

As with aircraft in the UK, from May 1942, the national markings of aircraft in the Middle East were changed to the new style, now being termed National marking I, (Red and Blue roundel on the upper surfaces of the mainplanes); National marking II, (Red, White and Blue roundel on the undersurfaces of the mainplanes); National marking III, (Red, White, Blue, and Yellow roundel on the fuselage sides); and Fin marking (i). The change over to these markings was a very gradual one spread over many months with both pre- and post-May 1942 types being seen until at least the end of the year.

Tank Busters

In the summer of 1942, the war in the Western Desert was approaching a critical phase. At this time Britain had a secret weapon in the shape of the Hurricane Mk IId with its two 40 mm 'S' guns. It had been created to fill the role of 'Tank Buster' as the British tanks of the time were found to be undergunned in comparison with German AFVs.

The Hurricanes of 6 Sqn which were the first squadron to be fitted with the 40 mm guns show an interesting variety of camouflage and marking schemes. The camouflage schemes appear to be a mix of Dark Earth and Middle Stone which by this time had been named the Desert Scheme, and Dark Green and Middle Stone of the Tropical Land Scheme with what appears to be Azure Blue under surfaces.

The national markings show a mix of pre- and post-May 1942 styles between different aircraft. For example BP131 is marked with the post-May 1942 style national markings, whilst BP188 is marked with the pre-May 1942 style, which would appear to indicate an inservice repaint.

The squadron markings are also of interest as they appear to be in Medium Sea Grey whilst the individual aircraft letter appears to be in Red. At least one aircraft, BP131, is known to have carried the Squadron's 'Flying can-opener' motif on the engine cowling.

Desert schemes

By October 1942, the camouflage requirements for Day Fighters abroad had been revised by an Air Ministry Order (AMO) once again. Now the upper surfaces were to be either the Day Fighter Scheme of Dark Green and Ocean Grey, the Temperate Land Scheme of Dark Green and Dark Earth or the Desert Scheme which was now defined as Dark Earth and Middle Stone.

Undersurfaces were to be, "Sky or azure". Whilst it is obvious that the reference to "azure" means Azure Blue, the reference to "Sky" is puzzling as this colour had been (a) rejected by Middle East Command over two years previously; and (b) also discontinued as an undersurface colour in the UK over a year previously. It is perhaps possible that what the AMO *meant* to say was "Sky Blue or Azure Blue" which would make a lot more sense in a Middle East context.

This interpretation is supported to some extent by a further revision to the AMO in December 1942 which states that the undersurfaces of Day Fighters abroad are to be "Sky, azure or light Mediterranean blue". This clearly implies that all three colours are shades of blue - ie Sky Blue, Azure Blue and Light Mediterranean Blue - and it is possible that this AMO was simply officially acknowledging what was already common practice on operational squadrons in the Middle East.

On occasion, squadrons serving in the Middle East which were manned by Allied or Commonwealth nations were allowed to modify the national markings of their aircraft to reflect the nationality of the squadron personnel. The two outstanding examples of this are the Squadrons of the Royal Hellenic Air Force and the South African Air Force

By December 1942 the squadrons of the RHAF had been authorised to apply a version of the Greek National marking roundel to their aircraft. The standard National marking I was retained on the upper surfaces of the mainplanes, but the National markings II and III; and the fin flash were Blue/White/Blue. No 335 Sqn which was equipped with Hurricanes is thought to be one of the squadrons marked in this way.

The squadrons of the South African Air Force also had their own variation of national markings. In their case, the Red centre of the roundel was replaced by an orange colour, presumably mixed on the squadrons by adding standard Yellow to Red?

During 1942, the Air Ministry ceased to issue two-letter squadron codes to overseas squadrons. This meant that a great many of the Hurricane squadrons in the Middle East did not carry them, being marked only with the individual aircraft letter. Such markings do not appear to have been as regulated as those applied in the UK. Hurricanes have variously been reported with White codes, Sky Blue codes, Red codes with a White outline, and Light Mediterranean Blue codes with a White outline.

Other squadrons, such as 73 and 274, are known to have carried multi-coloured 'flashes' on their Hurricanes' fuselage sides, but the colours of such markings are still by no means certain. The 73 Squadron flash for example is known to have been a different combination of colours on different aircraft, including Yellow, Night, White, Red, Blue, and light blue!

By May 1943, the war in North Africa had been won by the Allies who then began to contemplate a return to the European mainland via Southern Italy which meant that the Desert Scheme was to all intents and purposes surplus to requirements. In some respects this was just as well, as having so many different camouflage schemes in production was starting to cause 'problems' on the production lines.

The 'problems' came about because, at the time of manufacture, it was usually impossible to tell where in the world the aircraft would eventually serve. This meant that aircraft could be sent to an overseas Theatre wearing an entirely inappropriate camouflage scheme which then had to be altered before the aircraft could be issued to a squadron. Therefore the decision was taken at the end of 1943, that the camouflage and markings applied to all fighters would be those authorised for UK based aircraft. As far as the Hurricane was concerned, this meant that most of the final batch of Mk IIb, IIc and IVs, built between September 1943 and May 1944, would have been finished in the Day Fighter Scheme irrespective of where in the world they would eventually serve.

Above: Formation of No 6 Sqn 40mm 'S' gun armed Hurricane Mk IIds circa June 1942, perfectly illustrating the transition from the old to the new National markings styles - BP188 JV·Z in the old, and BP131 (behind) in the new.

Left: Hurricane Mk IIc, HL844, 'Sir Alasdair' (one of four Hurricanes presented by Lady MacRobert in memory of her sons), of 94 Sqn., based at El Gamil in 1942, in the standard Desert Scheme of Dark Earth and Middle Stone uppersurfaces with either Sky Blue, Azure Blue or Light Mediterranean Blue undersurfaces!

HURRICANE CAMOUFLAGE AND MARKINGS IN THE FAR EASTERN THEATRE OF OPERATIONS

When the Japanese launched their attack in the Far East on 7 December 1941, there were no Hurricanes at all in the region. Between the wars, Britain had assumed that there would be sufficient time to send a fleet to the Far East, which would be based at Singapore in order to deter any Japanese aggression. The war with Germany prevented this from happening, and it was only a matter of days before the Japanese attack that the first Hurricane squadron destined for the defence of Singapore, 242 Sqn, had been despatched. Nos 605, 232, and 258 Sqns which were already en route for other destinations were diverted to the Far East, arriving by 20 December.

Tropical schemes

The subsequent Japanese successes have all been well documented elsewhere, but unfortunately most of the RAF records of this period were destroyed and details of the camouflage and markings carried by the Hurricanes in the Far East during this period are scarce.

The instructions in force for the camouflage of aircraft for service abroad at this time specified that the upper surfaces were to be either Dark Green and Dark Earth or Dark Green and Middle Stone, according to the nature of the country in which they were to operate. Undersurfaces were to be Sky. The few photographs to have survived of the Hurricanes which fought over Singapore and the East Indies until March 1941 appear to show the Hurricanes to be fitted with tropical filters and camouflaged in both of these schemes. This should not be too surprising as the Hurricanes had been diverted from other destinations including some in the Middle East.

Other Squadrons were also diverted from the Middle East to the Far East such as 17, 135, and 136 Squadrons which were sent to Burma as 267 Wing. Of these squadrons, 17 Sqn is known to have had several Hurricanes which were finished in the Dark Green and Middle Stone scheme, (from the BE serial number range). The undersurfaces appear to have been a light colour. The fact that these aircraft had been diverted from the Middle East where Sky was considered unsuitable has already been discussed, and may be an indication that the undersurfaces of these aircraft were Sky Blue. These aircraft carried the Squadron's YB codes in Medium Sea Grey and also modified the roundels on the uppersurfaces of the mainplanes to the Red, White and Blue variety in what appears to be the then usual 1-3-5 proportions. It is not known whether this practice extended to the other squadrons in the Wing or exactly why it was done, but the most likely explanation is that the intention was to make the national marking more prominent and easily identified, especially in the light of subsequent events.

National markings changes

May 1942 saw the national markings change to the revised style National marking I, II, III and Fin marking (i), and eventually these markings found their way into service on Hurricanes in the Far East along with the Day Fighter Scheme which was now established on the UK-based production lines.

As has been previously mentioned, by October 1942 the camouflage requirements for Day Fighters abroad had been revised. Now the uppersurfaces were to be either the Day Fighter Scheme consisting of Dark Green and Ocean Grey; the Temperate Land Scheme of Dark Green and Dark Earth, or the Desert Scheme which was now defined as consisting of Dark Earth and Middle Stone - the implication from this is that the Dark Green and Middle Stone scheme had by now been taken out of production.

It has also been previously mentioned that undersurfaces were to be "Sky or azure" with all the confusing interpretations that this phrase is open to. Photographs of Hurricanes in the Far East tend to show a very light tone on their undersurfaces which might suggest the use of Sky Blue. The addition of Light Mediterranean Blue to the list of authorised undersurface colours in October 1942 serves to confuse the issue even more, but as this colour seems to reproduce as a comparatively dark tone in b&w photographs, it would appear to not have been used in the Far East.

Reducing the Red

From the outbreak of hostilities in the Far East in December 1941, the prominence of the Red centre in the RAF National marking had proved a problem as the Blue colour often faded to the point where at a distance it merged into the camouflage. As a result the Red centre became the most prominent feature of the marking, thus offering ample scope for misidentification. With the arrival of the American USAAF in India by April 1943, this problem had become acute following a number of errors in identification. The suggestion was made that perhaps the RAF National marking should be altered in some way so as to make British aircraft more easily recognised.

The solution was to adopt the same markings as used by the RAAF for exactly the same reason, eliminating the Red from the roundel entirely. Trials were put in hand to assess the new marking's suitability, during which it was discovered that the White centre in the new roundel was too prominent and compromised the camouflage of the aircraft. The solution was to mix a new off-white colour using four parts White and one part Blue, which was found to give a marking which was visible from 1,700 yards but did not compromise the aircraft's camouflage scheme. At the same time that the roundel was revised, the fin flash was also altered to off-white and Blue, with the off-white leading.

Two-tone Blue 'India' markings

Introduced from the end of June 1943, the new markings were originally sized in accordance with the provisions of the then current AMO, but after the Australians had been consulted about their markings, the RAF adopted the same proportions employed by the RAAF from about September 1943.

The new National markings were designed for three sizes of aircraft, small, medium, and large. Hurricanes, being single engine aircraft were classed as 'small' and therefore were to be marked with Blue roundels of 16 inches overall diameter with 6 inch diameter white centres and a flash 24 inches high and 16 inches wide divided into two 8 inch wide segments with the white leading.

South East Asia scheme

As mentioned in the previous section, by 1943, the profusion of colour schemes which could be applied to Hurricanes, and other types, destined for overseas

Right: A Langley-built Hurricane Mk IIc, LB835 'L' of No 34 Sqn., based in Burma in 1944, finished in the Day Fighter Scheme of Ocean Grey and Dark Green uppersurfaces with Medium Sea Grey undersides. The National markings are the two-tone blue 'India' style.

service was causing problems on the production line, as at the time of manufacture, it was usually impossible to tell where in the world the aircraft would eventually serve, which meant that aircraft could be sent to an overseas Theatre wearing an entirely inappropriate camouflage scheme which then had to be altered before the aircraft could be issued to a squadron.

This problem is illustrated by a Postagram sent from AHQ India to several Maintenance Units and Headquarters in India on 27 October 1943. Entitled 'Camouflage of Day Fighter Aircraft' the Postagram stated that some Hurricanes were being received into India camouflaged with the Desert Scheme and carrying UK identification markings with Yellow borders. These and other similar cases were to be re-camouflaged before despatch, in the Day Fighter Scheme with 'India' markings.

Details of the scheme were given as uppersurfaces in Dark Green and Ocean Grey with undersurfaces in Medium Sea Grey. Tactical markings included the Sky spinner and rear fuselage band and the Yellow strip along the leading edges of the wing. Squadron codes were to be Sky.

Within a month of these instructions being issued it had apparently been decided to accept any aircraft camouflaged in the Temperate Land Scheme as they were, and not re-camouflage them. Meanwhile back in the UK the decision was taken at the end of 1943 that the camouflage and markings applied to all fighters would be those authorised for UK based aircraft, so the supply of Hurricanes to the Far East in the Temperate Land Scheme would, in the fullness of time, dry up.

A return to Dark Earth

This was somewhat unfortunate, as over the next few months a rethink of the camouflage requirements for fighter aircraft in the Far East seems to have taken place and by April 1944 the Temperate Land Scheme of Dark Earth and Dark Green was the preferred camouflage scheme for use on the uppersurfaces, with Medium Sea Grey on the undersurfaces. This scheme was promulgated by an Air Force Order (India) in April 1944. The same order specified that no tactical markings were to be carried and the squadron codes were to be applied in Sky.

The final change in the colour scheme carried by Hurricanes in the Far East came with the introduction of Air Command South East Asia Special Identification Markings. On Hurricanes these took the form of a White spinner with a 28 inch wide band around the mainplanes and 18 inch wide bands around the tailplanes and fin.

When originally introduced on Hurricanes from 1 February 1945, the bands extended across the full chord of the mainplanes, tailplanes, fin and rudder. The Air Ministry was as ever concerned that this practice might upset the balance of the control surfaces and asked that the markings should not be applied over the ailerons, elevators and the rudder. By this time of course it was too late as many aircraft had already been marked up. As a consequence it is possible to find Hurricanes with the White markings extending across the full chord of wings and control surfaces, whilst on others the markings can be seen only on the fixed surfaces.

The Temperate Land Scheme of Dark Earth and Dark Green with Medium Sea Grey undersurfaces appears to have then remained in use on the Hurricanes in the Far East until the end of hostilities. When the Air Ministry enquired of the Overseas Commands which aircraft it would be permissible to operate without camouflage as part of the review of camouflage policy, which was being undertaken in early 1945, ACSEA cited the Hurricane as being the one fighter type for which camouflage was absolutely essential, although the exact reason for this is not known.

Far Eastern Photo Recce

Mention has already been made of the PR Hurricanes converted in Egypt. These Hurricanes are thought to have been camouflaged in a very dark blue colour which was even darker than the Blue used in the National markings. This colour is said to have been mixed from 5 gallons of an ICI colour called 'Bosun blue' to which was added 3lb Black pigment and 16lb of Zinc powder and turpentine. The resulting colour has been described as 'Royal blue' which was fractionally darker than FS 35109. The same colour is thought to have been applied to the Hurricane PR Mk IIs converted during late 1942 to early 1943, many of which subsequently went to No 3 PRU in India.

The first such aircraft are thought to have arrived in Rangoon in January 1942, carrying Red and Blue roundels on both wings and fuselage, defined with a 4 inch wide Yellow surround which reduced the diameter of the blue portion of the roundels. Serial numbers were applied in 4 inch high Night characters. Later deliveries were also camouflaged in the same shade of dark blue but the proportions of their markings differed from one Hurricane to another, although they remained the Red, Blue and Yellow variety. Some Hurricanes were delivered with National marking I, II, and III with their associated fin flash, but it is thought that the fuselage and fin markings were soon deleted so that the Hurricanes of 3 PRU only carried National markings on the wings with the serial number and individual aircraft letter on the fuselage.

Right: Hurri-bomber Mk IIcs, possibly of No 28 Sqn., early 1945, in the Temperate Land Scheme of Dark Earth and Dark Green uppersurfaces with Medium Sea Grey undersides. The white, Air Command South East Asia Special Identification Markings, can be seen around the mainplanes, tailplanes, across the top of the rudder and on the spinner.

HURRICANES AT SEA

As has already been recounted, the first Hurricanes to go to sea were those of 46 Squadron which had successfully landed on *HMS Glorious* at the end to the Norwegian campaign in June 1940, followed by the Hurricanes flown off *HMS Argus* to Malta in August 1940. However, these were not intended to play any role in air/sea warfare and towards the end of the Battle of Britain, a new threat to British shipping in the Atlantic emerged.

The threat was the Focke Wulf Fw 200 Condors of I./KG 40, flying from Bordeaux-Merignac in France, which began to fly long range patrols over the Western Approaches. As losses of shipping to these aircraft increased during October 1940, Britain began to investigate the feasibility of carrying an expendable fighter aircraft on a merchant ship which could be launched by catapult.

Merchant Ship Fighter Unit

The Hurricane was deemed to be suitable for this task and by January 1941 volunteer pilots were being sought to fly them. The unit responsible for operating these Hurricanes, the Merchant Ship Fighter Unit (MSFU) was formed at Speke in May 1941 with an eventual operational strength of approximately fifty Hurricanes. The Hurricanes, modified with catapult spools, were known as Sea Hurricane IAs and by the summer of 1941, they were in service on all the major convoy routes including those to the Soviet Union.

As far as is known, the catapult Hurricanes were camouflaged in the Temperate Sea Scheme on the upper surfaces, however, whilst the unit was in the process of receiving its first aircraft, it found that although it was receiving the correct number of parts to assemble the correct number of aircraft, the components were finished in a mixture of camouflage schemes! This led to some assembled aircraft having the wings in the Temperate Land Scheme for instance whilst the fuselages were finished in the Temperate Sea Scheme or vice versa! An appeal therefore was made to the Ministry of Aircraft Production (MAP) to supply Hurricanes in the Temperate Sea Scheme.

The Temperate Sea Scheme

The Temperate Sea Scheme had been invented by the Royal Aircraft Establishment at Farnborough in the mid 1930s as suitable for use over water and consisted of two colours for monoplanes called Extra Dark Sea Grey and Dark Slate Grey. The former colour was a dark bluish grey, whilst the latter was a dark green-grey.

Undersurfaces were to be Sky during 1941, but by 1942 however, there is the possibility that some MSFU Hurricanes had Medium Sea Grey undersurfaces as it is possible to see a distinct difference in tone between the undersurfaces and the tail band of some MSFU Hurricanes photographed in early 1942. National markings were the usual Red, White, Blue and Yellow in the 1-3-5-7 ratio up until May 1942 when they were changed to National marking I, II, III etc.

During the lifetime of the MSFU, the codes KE, LU, NJ and XS are thought to have been used. Exactly why so many different code combinations were used is unknown, but each combination may be linked to the operational detachments this unit maintained at Abbotsinch, Nova Scotia, Archangel and Gibraltar. These codes appear to have been applied in Sky. Serial numbers remained in Night. These markings appear to have remained in use until the MSFU disbanded in September 1943.

Sea Hurricanes

As the Royal Navy did not possess a modern deck landing fighter with a performance equal to the land based fighters of the day, it was perhaps only natural that the Hurricane should be navalised for operation from aircraft carriers. However, whilst it had proved relatively simple to install catapult spools in the Sea Hurricane IA, stressing the rear fuselage to allow the aircraft to be arrested after landing on an aircraft carrier was rather more difficult and it was not until September 1941 that the Sea Hurricane IB went into service. In the interim a number of FAA squadrons obtained standard Hurricanes from the RAF.

During 1940 it was decreed that all naval aircraft would be camouflaged on the upper surfaces in the Temperate Sea Scheme, and these colours were presumably applied to these Hurricanes. Undersurfaces were to be painted Sky. However, photographic evidence suggests that many of these Hurricanes might have retained their Temperate Land Scheme camouflage with a mix of 'A' and 'B'

Heading: Sea Hurricane Mk IBs of 885 Sqn aboard *HMS Victorious* in August 1942 just prior to 'Operation Pedestal'. The aircraft in the foreground is V7506 '7T' with yellow wing leading edges and fin and Sky codes, tailband and spinner. Note the post-May 1942 National markings.

Left: Sea Hurricane Mk IA, Z4936 KE•M of the Merchant Ship Fighter Unit, at Speke undergoing catapult trials. Camouflage scheme appears to be the Temperate Sea Scheme of Extra Dark Sea Grey and Dark Slate Grey uppersurfaces with either Sky or Medium Sea Grey undersides.

Left: An unidentified Sea Hurricane Mk IB - probably from a Training Unit aboard a Light Carrier - in the standard FAA Temperate Sea Scheme, to Pattern No 1, of Extra Dark Sea Grey and Dark Slate Grey uppersurfaces with Sky under surfaces.

Left below: Sea Hurricane Mk IIC, NF717, also in the Temperate Sea Scheme, but with post-May 1942 National markings. The orthochromatic film used, makes the Yellow outer ring to the National marking III on the fuselage appear to be very dark.

Schemes. Other Hurricanes do appear to have been refinished in the Temperate Sea Scheme colours on their upper surfaces and acquired Sky Grey under surfaces, which extended up the fuselage sides and the whole of the fin and rudder in the spring of 1941, to what became defined as Pattern No. 2.

By the time the Sea Hurricane Mk IB entered service though, the camouflage scheme seems to have settled down to be the Temperate Sea Scheme in the 'A' Scheme for the uppersurfaces and Sky to the standard lower demarcation Pattern No 1. Identification markings took the form of roundels in Red, White, Blue and Yellow as appropriate in the pre-May 1942 style, with squadron codes applied in Sky. The title 'Royal Navy' and the aircraft serial number was to be applied to the rear fuselage in 4 inch high characters in Night. Often, in late 1941, Sea Hurricanes could be seen sporting Sky spinners and tail bands which were identical to those carried on RAF Day Fighter aircraft.

Once the Temperate Sea Scheme to the 'A' Scheme was established in service with Sky undersurfaces to Pattern No 1, it seems to have remained unaltered until the end of the War.

'Operation Pedestal'

This attempt to 'fight' fourteen merchant ships through the Western Mediterranean to Malta in August 1942 was the biggest action fought by Sea Hurricanes. The aerial fighting lasted four days and at the end of it, just five ships including the now legendary tanker *Ohio* managed to get through at a critical time in the siege of Malta.

The Sea Hurricanes taking part in this action carried special recognition markings which consisted of Yellow wing leading edge stripes, from the landing lights out to the wing tip, and/or Yellow fins. At this time the markings were in a period of transition with the new National marking II and III with their associated fin flash which had been introduced in May 1942 starting to make an appearance. Whilst most of the Sea Hurricanes retained their Sky Spinners, some no longer carried the Sky tail bands and a few aircraft could be seen sporting the new red codes. Most codes however appear to still have been marked in Sky at this stage. The usual 'Royal Navy' title and aircraft serial number appeared in the usual place on the rear fuselage.

In addition to these markings, the aircraft of 800 Sqn carried a white band around the nose just behind the spinners which were Night. These markings appear to have been already in place prior to 'Operation Pedestal'. The other anomaly in the markings carried by this squadron was that they carried their squadron code (the numeral '6') and individual aircraft letter on the leading edges of the wing root. The individual aircraft letter, which appears to have been applied in Sky, was restricted to the fuselage sides.

'Operation Torch'

During 'Operation Torch' in November 1942, the National markings on the Sea Hurricanes taking part were altered. The roundels on both sides of the wings and the fuselage were repainted to consist of a white five pointed star on a blue background inside a yellow ring which gave the Hurricanes a distinctly 'American' appearance. This was done to avoid confusion amongst the American forces who were unfamiliar with either British or French aircraft and could not be relied upon to know one from the other. It would appear that besides altering the National markings, squadron codes may also have been painted out. The 'Royal Navy' titles and serial numbers remained on the aircraft however.

Squadron code colours

During 1942, the colour used by first line squadrons for their codes was changed to 'dull red' and second line squadrons to Yellow. There apparently remains some debate as to what exactly was meant by 'dull red'. Some colour photographs suggest that this colour was more 'dull' (ie darker), than the red used in the roundel, whilst other colour photographs show the shade of red being used in the codes to be identical to that in the roundel. At the time of writing nothing more is known about this anomaly and

Right: Sea Hurricane Mk IBs of 800 and 880 Sqn aboard *HMS Indomitable* circa August 1942, during the 'Operation Pedestal' period. The Sea Hurricane in the foreground is Z4550 6·G, (although only the individual letter 'G' is applied to the fuselage - the full code appearing on the inboard leading edges of the mainplanes), with a white band around the nose just behind the spinner. AF955, 7·E, of 880 Sqn., immediately behind the lead aircraft, carries its full codes but only on the fuselage sides. It also has a Sky tail band and black checks on part of its white nose band.

Left: One of the losses during 'Operation Torch', was this 12-gun Sea Hurricane Mk XII, JS327 from *HMS Biter*, which crash-landed at St Leu near Algiers on 8 November 1942. Note the white 'Torch' stars applied over the roundels and encircled by a yellow ring, and the painted out fin flash.

Below Sea Hurricane Mk IBs of 885 Sqn aboard *HMS Victorious*, showing the red 'front line' Squadron codes introduced in mid-1942 and retention of the RAF 'Fighter Command' style Sky tail band. The aircraft in the foreground, coded 7U, carries post-May 1942 National markings, whilst the aircraft in front of 7U, coded 7Y, still has the previous 1-3-5-7 ratio style.

the best we can do is say that squadron codes were red.

'Operation Torch' marked the beginning of the end of the Sea Hurricane's service from Fleet Aircraft Carriers. By this date even the Mk IIC was no match for its land based counterparts and their place was taken by such types as the Martlet, Hellcat, Corsair, and Seafire. This however did not prevent Sea Hurricanes remaining in service until the end of the war in a number of second line squadrons and even on board Escort Carriers where they would not normally expect to meet land based fighters.

There were few changes in the marking of Sea Hurricanes during the rest of the war. The National marking I on the upper surfaces of the wings was supposed to be changed to National marking IA from January 1945, and from April, the squadron codes were once again to be applied in Sky on operational aircraft but remained Yellow on second line aircraft.

Having said that, Flag Officers had the authority to authorise local modifications both to the camouflage schemes and tactical markings, provided that the Commanders of other British and Allied services in the area and the Admiralty were notified.

Probably the best known example of a local modification of camouflage ever applied to Sea Hurricanes was 835 Sqn aboard *HMS Nairana* in June 1944 whilst employed on convoy escort work Their Sea Hurricane IICs carried a spectacular colour scheme which rendered the aircraft almost entirely white overall. The only part of the aircraft which was not white was the extreme top of the engine cowling from the windscreen down to the spinner, which appears to have been left in the upper surface camouflage colours of Extra Dark Sea Grey/Dark Slate Grey.

The identification markings also varied slightly from the then current Admiralty Fleet Order, as the Red/Blue National marking I was retained on the upper surface of the mainplanes and the Red squadron and individual aircraft markings were carried on the side of the fuselage in the usual places. Otherwise the aircraft appear to have been correctly marked with the Red/White/Blue National marking II under the wings, Red/White/Blue/Yellow National marking III on the fuselage sides and Fin marking (i) being retained, as were the 'Royal Navy' titles and serial number in Night. A Squadron badge was carried on a shield under the canopy on the starboard side of the fuselage.

This scheme would appear to have been based upon the Anti-Submarine scheme then in use by both the RAF and FAA, but there would appear to be no evidence to suggest that this was fully executed on the Sea Hurricanes to the extent of finishing the under surfaces to Pattern No 1 in Gloss White and to Pattern No 2 in Matt White. The available photographs suggest that Matt White was used throughout.

Left: Sea Hurricane Mk IIC, NF700 7•T of 835 Sqn aboard *HMS Nairana*, summer 1944, in the overall white scheme peculiar to this unit's Sea Hurricanes.